Dion For...

APPLIED MAGIC
and
ASPECTS OF OCCULTISM

Dion Fortune's

APPLIED MAGIC
and
ASPECTS OF OCCULTISM

THE AQUARIAN PRESS

This edition first published 1987

British Library Cataloguing in Publication Data

Fortune, Dion
[Applied magic]. Dion Fortune's Applied magic; and, Aspects of occultism.
1. Occult sciences
Rn: Violet Mary Firth   I. [Applied magic]
II. Title   III. Fortune, Dion. Aspects of occultism
133   BF1411

ISBN 0-85030-665-5

The Aquarian Press is part of the Thorsons Publishing Group, Wellingborough, Northamptonshire, NN8 2RQ, England.

Printed in Great Britain by Woolnough Bookbinding Limited, Irthlingborough, Northamptonshire.

3 5 7 9 10 8 6 4

Contents

Preface

The works of the late Dion Fortune were written a long time ago and since then a great deal more has been understood and realized so that many of the ideas then expressed are not now necessarily acceptable. Also, much of what she wrote was written from the viewpoint of the psychic. Psychism is simply one type of inner awareness and there are other types at least as valid and as common. Non-psychic readers, therefore, can translate experience in terms of psychic imagery into terms of their own inner awareness.

The publication of these books continues at present because there is still much of value in them and because they can act as valuable pointers to seekers.

Details of the aims and work of the Society of the Inner Light, founded by Dion Fortune, may be obtained by writing (with postage please) to the Secretary at 38 Steele's Road, London NW3 4RG, England.

In December 1942 Dion Fortune wrote:

There are things I wrote of *Spiritualism* twenty years ago which, in the light of wider experience, I would not write today, and to cite these as evidence against me is to deny the possibility of human progress.

PART ONE
APPLIED MAGIC

1.

The Occult Way

The Mystic Way that leads to Divine Union is so well known that it is often forgotten that there is another Path, seemingly totally different in route, that leads in the end to the same goal. We are so accustomed to hear the renunciation of the world and the abnegation of the self set up as the only true Path of the sould which seeks the Highest, that we hardly dare whisper that there may be. another Path—the Path of the mastery of manifested existence and the apotheosis of the self.

There are two ways in which God can be worshipped; we can worship Him in unmanifested Essence, or we can worship Him in His manifested form. Both ways are legitimate, provided that in worshipping the manifested form we do not forget the Essence, and in worshipping the Essence we do not confuse it with the manifested form, for these things are the sin of idolatry, which consists in a wrongly-placed emphasis.

The mystic seeks to worship God in essence. But the essence or root of God, being unmanifest, eludes human consciousness. The mystic, then, in order to conceive the object of his worship, has to transcend normal human consciousness. It is not possible to know the inmost nature of a state of existence unless we can enter into it and share, in some measure at least, its experience. The Mystic, then, has for his task the freeing of his consciousness from its habitual bondage to form. It is to this end that the ascetic discipline is directed, killing out the lower in order that the higher may be set free to unite with God and thereby know Him. The Way of the Mystic is a way of renunciation till he breaks all the limitations of his lower nature and enters into his freedom; nothing then remains that can withhold him from God, and his soul flies upwards to enter the Light and return not again.

But the other Path is not a way of Renunciation, but a Way of Fulfilment; it is not a breaking away from the path of human destiny, but a concentration and sublimation of that destiny. Each soul which takes that Path lives through its own experience every phase and aspect of manifested existence and equilibrates it, spiritualizes it, and absorbs its essence.

The aim of those who follow this Path is to obtain complete mastery over every aspect of created life. But when we say mastery, we do not mean the mastery of a slave-owner over his slave. Rather do we mean the mastery of the virtuoso over his instrument; a mastery which rests upon his power to adapt himself to its nature and enter into its spirit and so draw forth its full capacity of interpretation. The adept who has gained mastery over the Sphere of Luna interprets the message of the Moon to the world and shows forth her powers in equilibrated balance. The kingdom ruled by the Master of the Temple is no absolute monarchy. He does not obtain that mastery in order to make thrones, dominions and powers serve himself, but in order to bring to them God's message of salvation and call them to their high heritage. He is a servant of evolution; it is his task to bring order out of chaos, harmony out of discord, and reduce unbalanced forces to equilibrium.

The Vedanta teaching of the Eastern Tradition clearly distinguishes between the devotion to the Unmanifest God, the spiritual essence of creation, and the manifesting aspects, or gods. 'Identify the self with the partial aspects, which are the Yoginis, and the various Powers (Siddhis) are attained. Identify the self with the Maha-yogini Herself, and man is liberated, for he is no longer man but Her. . . . With what a man should identify himself depends upon what he wants. But whatever it is, he gets the Power if he but will and works for it.' (*World as Power, Power as Reality*, by Woodroffe.)

What ought a man to want? That is the next question we have to ask ourselves. The answer to this depends entirely upon the stage of evolution we have arrived at. The soul has to complete its human experience before it is ready for Divine Union. It must pass the nadir of the descent into matter before it can come on to the Path of Return. We are not ready for the Mystic Way until we are approaching the time of our freedom from the Wheel of Birth and Death; to try and escape from that Wheel prematurely is to evade our training. Like the racing yacht which fails to round the outermost marking-buoy, we are disqualified; we have not fulfilled the conditions of liberation, which command that we shall shirk nothing and leave behind us only that which we have mastered, equilibrated, and outgrown.

It is a false teaching which bids us eradicate from our natures anything which God has implanted there, as false and foolish as ham-stringing a spirited thorough-bred colt because it is wild and unbroken. The love of beauty, the vitalizing urge of clean, normal, healthy instinct, the joy of battle, we should be poor creatures indeed without all these. God gave them to us, and we may presume that He knew what He was about when He did so. Who are we to judge His handiwork and condemn that which He found good?

What God's law forbids is the abuse of these things, not the use for the purposes for which they are intended. The Path of the Hearth-fire gives a far sounder and more effectual discipline of the instincts than the hermit-caves of Thebes, with their ascetic tortures and self-mutilations, doing violence to Nature and outraging God's handiwork.

Frightened by the Elemental forces when he meets them unpurified and unprepared, the ascetic flees from what he believes to be temptation. It is a far sounder policy to equilibrate the warring forces in our own nature until we can handle our unruly team of instincts and make them draw the chariot of the soul with the power of their untiring speed.

The day will come for each one of us when we shall be freed from the Wheel of Birth and Death and enter the Light to return not again; if we try to put aside the Elements and their problems before that day dawns we are shifting our helm for the homeward course before we have rounded the marking-buoy; we are like the man who buried his talent in the ground because he was afraid of it. Our Lord will not thank us for our misplaced devotion to an unripe ideal, but call us unprofitable servants.

The key to the whole problem, like so many others, lies in the doctrine of reincarnation. If we believe that all human achievement has to be accomplished in one life and that at the end of it we shall be judged, we are liable to be stampeded into an idealism which we have not yet attained by a process of natural growth. Freedom from the Wheel, the abandonment of matter, Divine Union—these will come for all of us in due course of evolutionary time, for it is the aim of evolution to bring us to them, but that time may not be yet, and we are very foolish if we allow another, however advanced, to judge for us where we stand upon the ladder of evolution, and decide what is to be our next step. Let us have the courage of our convictions and follow our own deeper promptings. If our urge is to worship God in His glorious manifestation, let us do it wholeheartedly; therein lies the way of attainment for us. This does not mean the unleashing of the impulses; the Dance of Nature is an ordered and rhythmical movement, we must not break from our place in the living pattern or we will spoil it. We must work with Nature for Nature's ends if She is to be our Mother. Here is discipline enough for any soul.

If, on the other hand, our promptings are towards a withdrawal on to the Mystical Path, let us ask ourselves honestly whether we are following that Path because the call of God in our hearts is so strong, or because we have found life so difficult that we want to escape for ever from its problems.

2.

Some Practical Applications of Occultism

When I first came to the study of Occult Science, it was extremely hidden and secretive. The various open societies that existed were either purely exoteric and elementary, or else they were really quite bogus. So it was difficult to know where to look for any real teaching. Consequently, unless one were psychic one was completely debarred from any knowledge. But this is no longer so in the same degree, and the problem remains for many people, do they want the occult teaching or not? We are so accustomed to think that in order to have any practical knowledge of occultism one must go apart from the world, and it is not practicable for the vast majority of people to follow that path at all. That meant that a very great many people who could have had great help from this teaching were debarred from pursuing its study, which I think is a pity. When I was training it was a strenuous affair altogether. The more I see of it, the more I feel that the work of the adept is one thing, and the general giving out of the teaching is another. The feats which are done by the trained gymnast are entirely beyond the scope of the ordinary man; but nevertheless, the same exercises on which the gymnast is trained, only not carried to the same extreme pitch, keep the ordinary man strong and fit when practised regularly. So I think it is with Occultism. If you want to be an adept and do the strong feats of Magic, you are equivalent to the gymnast, and this means a very strenuous training. But I think the next application of this work will be the bringing of the teachings, so that they are available for people not able to leave all, whose Karma holds them to daily life. It is interesting to note that at the time when the recrudescence of occultism began in the West—about 1875—three movements had their inception: Occultism, the Spiritualist Movement, and Christian Science, with New Thought as its offspring. These are three distinct lines dealing with occult forces. The occultist bases his work on tradition and generally uses ceremonial. The spiritualist is approaching the same ground, but has no tradition and bases his

work on experiment. The Christian Scientist has no tradition or
experiment, but bases his work on the hypothesis of the powers of the
mind. Spiritualism and Christian Science are rule-of-thumb procedures.
If one studies the healing movement of Christian Science one sees that
it has a very good method, but its practitioners seldom can explain it.
Occultism is the scientific basis of all these movements and can explain
the phenomena of these different modes of experience and practice.
In that its value lies. Christian Science and New Thought do yield valuable
fruits, but they give no explanation that a thinking person can accept,
and yet they get their results. Therefore find that basis, and do not away
with the valuable results. I maintain that in the esoteric doctrines we
get an explanation of so much in life that everybody would be richer
for having them given. Life is a very different matter if we have a clue
to its meaning. Without this we are like leaves blown in the wind, we
do not know where we are or where we are going; we are blind and
wandering as best we may, groping our way, with no guarantee that we
do not fall over a precipice. But if we take the esoteric doctrines, then
we see ourselves as part of the great whole.

We see our place in Nature, we see whence we have come and where
we are going, and we see our relationship to the Cosmos, and the whole
of life opens up. That is what esoteric science can give—a very broad,
profound and practical application of occultism. My experience with
many esoteric scientists is this—they make a sort of intellectual study
of it, but they do not apply it to practical problems. They are more or
less engaged in research work, in studying symbol systems, the Qabalah,
etc., but except as a means for divination these studies are for them
of no practical application to life. Moreover these divinations are very
spurious on the whole and tend to demoralize people's outlook on life.
If something good or bad is going to happen to a person shortly, what
good does it do to tell them so? But they can find the explanation of
things in an interpretation of life. When we study the esoteric teachings
of evolution, we see a tremendous vista opening up before us. And of
course the belief in reincarnation is implicit in occultism, as is that in
thought-transference. There we have, I think, one of the most illuminating
teachings that can possibly be given to the problems of life. What can
any being do in one life to earn either Heaven or Hell for ever? Surely
the teaching of reincarnation is a more reasonable one—the going out
and returning again, and going out once more into incarnation for further
experience. That is to my mind a very wonderful concept of existence—
that behind us stretches a long chain of incarnations. We do not remember

them because the memory chain is broken, but they are there, and the Divine Spark is the core of each one of us, round which experience has built up a whole; this constitutes the temperament and capacities of each one of us. That concept gives us a very deep philosophy of life. If the fortunes of life are blind hazard, then indeed we are most miserable. But if we see that the broad outlines of the spiritual experiences that life brings us are determined by our own soul, we shall begin to see how to take things.

Then comes another question—the great esoteric doctrine of the invisible planes of existence. These teachings tell us that what the five senses see or contact does not constitute the whole of existence. This exoteric science can confirm, by means of the microscope, etc. But the occultist goes further and says there is a whole kingdom of mind and spirit as well, which you do not see with your physical senses. In these live the great Forces which actuate life and its circumstances. In it you will find the key to conditions of life on the physical plane, and you will never find it anywhere else. Such people as Coué are manipulating these invisible forces successfully. If we understand these conditions, we shall be free, we shall then be able to work with these forces and manipulate them ourselves. But we can manipulate them only within very definite limits. Christian Science sets no limits; but if we watch the results they obtain, we can see that there are limits. There are certain things you are wise not to meddle with. The occultist does not try to dominate Nature, but to bring himself into harmony with these great Cosmic Forces, and work with them. You can see an illustration of this if you watch the Thames bargees pushing off when the tide is on the turn; they are taking advantage of their knowledge of the tides, and the river does the rest. With us in life, we should have the same knowledge and wisdom. We ought to understand these natural laws of the Unseen. They are *natural* laws, and there is nothing spooky about them. We can make life a very different thing if we do understand them. Of course, there are certain conditions we must accept, that are the fruits of Karma; but I do not want you to take Karma in the crude way in which it is sometimes put forth. It is not a question of murder for murder, that if you steal from a person in this life, that same person will steal from you in the next. It is not as simple as that. It means that something in your nature has got to be realized and changed so that you shall be in harmony. As long as that particular factor is in your nature, it will precipitate a similar sort of trouble in your life. Errors of intention, deliberate wrong-doing, are usually paid for in future lives; you may get away with it in this life—we have all seen the wicked flourish like a green bay tree—but the effect of that goes on, it is put down to your account, and in due time you have got to pay. But payment is always in spiritual values. You learn that you have got to make certain adjustments, and when you have done this, the pressure eases up, and you are free. So point by point we gain character and equilibrium. We win our freedom by learning the lessons life forces on us; and if we refuse, they become more and more drastic. When people have arrived at a certain degree of development, they are more sensitive and have more spiritual force, and so their problems are more acute. The soul may have decided to go rapidly on, and brings down in a concentrated form all the Karma due. Trouble seems always to come down on this soul, and through an incarnation of trouble the soul is purified, and then the next incarnation opens up free of these conditions. A single incarnation does not furnish us with a clue, but leaves us with a sense of injustice; but if we see all our past lives stretching out, we see differently. We should always look at things in the light of three lives. And we can achieve our purposes in three lives too. We are making the conditions for our next life now, though in the present we have to take all or part of the Karma left from our last one. Some people say, 'Surely one life is trying enough.' But there is another way to look at it. If we average out our troubles against the long aeons of all our lives, they take on a different proportion. A great sense of freedom comes to the soul when the actual realization comes that the 'I' is going on, and that this incarnation is but an incident in its career. We cannot give anybody that freedom by simply explaining the logical grounds; but a sudden realization comes of something that has been before, and this causes a great alteration of life's values. Again, if we inspect our life's problems we may find it may be because we are working things out rapidly and developing fast. We say: 'This is the material condition that afflicts us, therefore we needed it, and we must learn the lessons it came to give.' We try to interpret the spiritual significance of this experience. Let us develop our souls by meditation on it. When the soul has acquired this quality or learnt the lesson that it needed to learn, then the Karmic burden is lifted. When people tackle their conditions they do not change until the freedom is won. We think we would be happy if only certain things were changed; but no, the conditions are in ourselves, and would only bring other similar conditions back. When I was working in a nerve clinic we saw this happen over and over again. The same sort of trouble kept recurring in the same life. There was one woman who had been attacked by tramps three or four

times in her life. This does not happen to everyone in the ordinary course
of things. Or again, a woman may be continually falling under the power
of a bully and be treated with cruelty—first a father, then a husband,
and then in her work. We see one particular form of trouble recurring
again and again in one person's life. There must be something which
determines the recurring experience. If we, most of us, look back through
our own lives we can see this to some extent at least. There must be
some prominent factor in our own make-up which draws from the
invisible forces. The only way to deal with these is by changing your
character by meditation, by building thought-forms or by deliberately
destroying what we call the thought-forms which are the channels of
the undesirable things towards you. These are the practical applications
of Occultism, and we do not need to be adepts to apply these.

We are making thought-forms one way or the other all the time. Our
thoughts not only influence us, they form channels of ingress and attract
the corresponding forces in the Cosmos itself. If you surround yourself
with hate-thoughts, you will be attracting a sort of Cosmic hate to yourself.
The occultist has a system of labelling these forces, he works all these
things out. We have such a system in the Qabalistic Tree of Life and
the beliefs underlying it can be very valuable in life; they teach the
tremendous power of mind and the strict limits in which it works, with
which we can do so much. These doctrines should leaven thought more
and more. The Theosophical Society has done a big work in this way,
but its appeal has been chiefly to the unorthodox and the rebel. This
is a great loss, because these teachings should be and can be presented
in such a way that they do not estrange the trained mind, which in pure
science is indispensable. Modern physics is coming completely round
to the occult teachings. The things that Blavatsky said and was laughed
to scorn for, are now becoming a matter of pure physics. There are great
applications of these things which must be made. They should be applied
to Sociology, to the administration of the prison and the asylum, where
the thought-forms set up re-infect people unless we neutralize them.
We can consider its practical applications to medicine, of which it has
the only real keys. If you deal with man as body only, it is very
unsatisfactory. Equally, if we take the orthodox view and deal with man
as a spirit only, we are not doing him justice. Auto-intoxication and sin
are different. Man is a fourfold being, and you must deal with him as
such. You must discern on which level the trouble originates. The life
forces of the spiritual level are the real keys to the whole problem, and
these life-forces are translated through the intellect and the understanding

and brought down the planes.

These are some of the esoteric teachings by which anyone can profit. I think the great need of occult secrecy is mainly past, but some is still necessary. Partly because a group mind is necessary for some forms of practical occultism, and this has to be conserved, and not dissipated as is done if a thing is common property and knowledge; and also to safeguard individuals against popular prejudice. Madame David-Neel, in her books about Tibet, has told us that there is no secrecy about the *teachings* of the Lamas and the inner wisdom there. The things that *are* kept secret are the practical methods of training their students. She herself in her books has given out many teachings which are important keys to the understanding of many occult doctrines. There are no mysteries about the teachings, but only about the practical methods, with which people could do harm. So we see that the practical work of occultism can be done only by trained minds and requires a high degree of training; but the principles can be most valuable and the more these are given out the better.

3.

The Group Mind

The term Group Mind is sometimes used loosely among occultists as if it were interchangeable with Group Soul. The two concepts are, however, entirely distinct. The Group Soul is the raw material of mind-stuff out of which individual consciousness is differentiated by experience; the Group Mind is built up out of the contributions of many individualized consciousnesses concentrating upon the same idea.

Let us take a concrete instance to make this clear. During the height of his popularity Marshal Joffre visited England and was accorded a great ovation. While driving from his hotel to the Mansion House to be received by the Lord Mayor his car passed through many streets. Individuals recognized him and stared, but no demonstration was made. But when he came to the crowded Mansion House crossing, policemen held up the traffic, saluting; the crowd saw that something was afoot; he was recognized, his name passed from mouth to mouth, and in a moment there was a wave of wildest enthusiasm. Self-contained, placid people were lifted and carried away by the wave of excitement, and found themselves shouting and waving their hats like maniacs. Note the difference between the behaviour of the crowd when it functioned as a crowd from the behaviour of isolated individuals, however numerous, who merely stared with interest, but displayed no emotion.

This incident brings to mind another Mansion House incident very illustrative of crowd psychology and the group mind. Many years ago Abdul Hamed, the detested Sultan of Turkey, visited England. He too was received by the Lord Mayor and drove to the Mansion House. Exactly the same scenes were repeated but with a different emotional content. He drove in safety through the crowded streets, individuals staring open-mouthed at the notorious visitor, but making no demonstration; but when the traffic was held up for him at the Mansion House crossing the crowd recognized him, from those quiet, sober, middle-aged City men there went up a howl of execration like the cry of a pack of wolves, the crowd surged forward as one man, and it was with the greatest difficulty that he was saved from being dragged from his carriage.

Which of those individual City men, unadventurous clerks content with their desks, would have assaulted the aged and august Abdul Hamed single-handed? Yet when caught up in the wave of crowd emotion they were capable of making a savage attack amid a babel of animal snarlings. For the moment something like an obsessing entity took possession of the souls of all and each; a vast Something, of a character which was not the sum of the mass of the individual souls, but vaster, more potent, more fiercely and vividly alive and conscious of its impulses. Yet at ordinary times the thronging crowds at the Mansion House crossing go each their own way, absorbed in their own thoughts, indifferent to, oblivious of their neighbours. What was it that turned this mass of hurrying, indifferent units into a united band uplifted by the enthusiasm of an ideal, or an organism capable of dangerous violence?

The key to the whole situation lies in the direction of the attention of a number of people to a common object about which they all feel strongly in the same way. Direction of attention to a common object without emotion does not have the same effect. The electric signs of Piccadilly Circus, though crowds stand and watch them, do not cause the formation of a group mind.

With these data to assist us, let us consider the problem in its occult applications. What is this strange oversoul that forms and disperses so swiftly when a number of people are of one mind in one place? For an explanation we must consider the theory of Artificial Elementals.

An Artificial Elemental is a thought-form ensouled by Elemental essence. That essence may be drawn directly from the Elemental kingdoms or it may be derived from the magician's own aura. A thought-form built up by continual visualizing and concentration, and concerning which a strong emotion is felt, becomes charged with that emotion and is capable of an independent existence outside the consciousness of its creator. This is a very important factor in practical occultism, and the explanation of many of its phenomena.

Exactly the same process that leads to the formation of an artificial Elemental by a magician takes place when a number of people concentrate with emotion on a single object. They make an artificial Elemental, vast and potent in proportion to the size of the crowd and the intensity of its feelings. This Elemental has a very marked mental atmosphere of its own, and this atmosphere influences most powerfully the feelings of every person participating in the crowd emotion. It gives them telepathic suggestion, sounding the note of its own being in their ears and thereby reinforcing the emotional vibration which originally gave it birth; there is action and reaction, mutual stimulus and intensification, between the Elemental and its makers. The more the crowd concentrates upon its object of emotion, the vaster the Elemental becomes; the vaster it becomes, the stronger the mass suggestions it gives to the individuals composing the crowd that created it; and they, receiving this suggestion, find their feelings intensified. Thus it is that mobs are capable of deeds of passion from which every individual member would shrink with horror.

. A mob Elemental, however, disperses as rapidly as it forms because a mob has no continuity of existence; the moment the stimulus of a common emotion is removed, the mob ceases to be a unit and reverts to heterogeneity. That is why undisciplined armies, however enthusiastic, are unreliable fighting machines; their enthusiasm evaporates if it is not continually stimulated; they split up into their component parts of many individuals with diversified interests, each activated by the instinct of self-preservation. To build up a group mind of any endurance some method of ensuring continuity of attention and feeling is essential.

Whenever such continuity of attention and feeling has been brought about, a group mind, or group Elemental, is formed which with the passage of time develops an individuality of its own, and ceases to be dependent for its existence upon the attention and emotion of the crowd that gave it brith. Once this occurs, the crowd no longer possesses the power to withdraw its attention or to disperse; the group Elemental has it in its grip. The attention of each individual is attracted and held in spite of himself; feelings are stirred within him even if he does not wish to feel them.

Each newcomer to the group enters into this potent atmosphere, and either accepts it, and is absorbed into the group, or rejects it, and is himself rejected. No member of a group with a strong atmosphere, group mind, or Elemental (according to which term we prefer), is at liberty to think without bias upon the objects of group concentration and emotion. It is for this reason that reforms are so hard to bring about.

The vaster the organization that needs reforming, the harder it is to move, and the stronger must be the personality that attempts the task. Yet once that forceful personality has begun to make an impression he speedily finds that a group is gathering under his leadership, and that this in its turn is developing an Elemental, and the momentum he has originated has begun to push him along. When he flags in his leadership the movement he created forces him forward. The solitary individual may turn aside and pause in moments of doubt and discouragement; not so the leader of a strongly emotionalized group; as soon as he slacks his pace he feels the pressure of the group mind behind him and it carries him forward during his hours of weakness and darkness. It may also, if his scheme has been unwisely conceived, carry him away and dash him to pieces on the rocks of a misjudged policy, a policy of which he would have seen the unwisdom if he had considered the matter rationally. There is no stopping the momentum of a movement which is moving along the lines of evolution. The group mind of the participants forms a channel for the manifestation of the forces of evolution, and the momentum developed is irresistible. But however potent the personality, however vast the resources, however popular the catch-phrases, if the movement is contrary to cosmic law it is only a matter of time till the whole group rushes madly down a steep slope into the sea. For in such a case it is the very momentum that is worked up which is the cause of its destruction. Give a false movement enough rope and it will always hang itself, falling by its own weight when that has grown sufficiently top-heavy to overbalance it.

This factor of the Group Mind is an exceedingly important key to the understanding of human problems, and explains the irrationality of men in mass. There are some very interesting books upon this subject, notably, *The Psychology of the Herd in Peace and War* by Wilfred Trotter, and *The Group Mind* by William McDougal. These will well repay study for the light they throw upon the problems of everyday life and human nature. The occultist carries the practical application of the doctrine of group minds much further than does the psychologist. In it he finds the key to the power of the Mysteries. Considered with an understanding of crowd psychology, it becomes obvious that the method of the Mysteries and the secret fraternities of all ages is based upon practical experience of its facts. What could be more conducive to the formation of a powerful group mind than the secrecy, the special costume, the processions and chantings of an occult ritual? Anything which differentiates a number of individuals from the mass and sets them apart forms a group mind automatically. The more a group is segregated, the greater the difference between it and the rest of mankind, the stronger is the group mind thus engendered. Consider the strength of the group mind of the Jewish race, set apart by ritual, by manners, by temperament and by persecution. There is nothing like persecution to give vitality to a group mind. Very truly is the blood of martyrs the seed of the Church, for it is the cement of the group mind.

It is for this reason that the secrecy of the Mysteries will never be entirely abrogated. However much is given out, something must always be kept in reserve and secret, because this something which, unshared with others and the focus of the attention of the group, is the nucleus of the group mind, the focus of its attention; it is to the group mind what the grain of sand is to the pearl forming within the oyster. If there were no grain of sand there would be no pearl. Remove that which differentiates the initiate from the rest of men and the group mind of which he forms a part will fall to pieces.

The potency of ceremonial, physically performed, does not rest only in its appeal to the entity invoked but also in its appeal to the imaginations of the participants. An adept, working alone, will work a ritual in picture consciousness on the astral without moving from his meditation posture, and this ritual will be effective for the purposes of invocation. But if he wants to make an atmosphere in which the development of his pupils will advance as in a forcing-house, or if he wishes to raise his own consciousness beyond its normal limitations, transcending his own will power and unaided vision, he will make use of the powers of the group Elemental developed by ritual.

This group mind, or ritual Elemental, acts upon the participants in the ceremony in exactly the same way as the mob emotion acted upon the peaceful City men when they saw Marshal Joffre. They are lifted out of themselves; they are more than human for the moment, for a group Elemental, formed of the appropriate emotion, is just as capable of raising consciousness to the level of the angels as of lowering it to the level of the beasts.

When our emotion goes out strongly towards an object, we are pouring out a subtle but nevertheless potent form of force. If that emotion is not a mere blind outpouring, but formulates itself into the idea of doing something, and especially if that idea causes a dramatic mental picture to rise in the mind, the outpouring force is formulated into a thought-form; the mental picture is ensouled by the outpoured force and becomes an actuality upon the astral. This thought-form itself now begins to give off vibrations, and these vibrations, by the law of the sympathetic induction of vibration, tend to reinforce the feelings of the person whose emotion gave rise to them and to induce similar feelings in others present whose attention is directed to the same object, even if they have hitherto been disinterested onlookers.

It will be seen that the theory of the group mind is now being associated with the doctrine of auto-suggestion as formulated by Baudouin, and these two established psychological concepts are extended by association with the esoteric concept of telepathy. Take these three factors together and we have the key not only to the phenomena of mob psychology, but also to the little realized power of ritual, especially ritual as it is performed in an occult lodge.

Let us consider what happens when such a ritual is performed. All present have their attention riveted upon the drama of the presentation of the ceremony. Every object within the range of their vision is symbolic of the idea that is being expressed by the ceremony. No circumstance that can heighten the concentration and the emotion is neglected. Consequently a highly concentrated and highly energized group is built up.

As we have already seen, when one thinks of any object with emotion force is poured forth. If a number of people are thinking of the same object with emotion, their attention concentrated and their feelings exalted by the ritual of the ceremony, they are pouring into a common pool no inconsiderable measure of subtle force. It is this force which forms the basis of the manifestation of whatever potency is being invoked.

In religions where the gods or the saints are freely represented in pictorial form, the imaginations of the worshippers are accustomed to picturing them as they have seen them represented; whether it be the hawk-headed Horus or the Virgin Mary. When a number of devout worshippers are gathered together, their emotions concentrated and exalted by ritual, and all holding the same image in imagination, the outpoured force of all present is formed into an astral simulacrum of the being thus intensely pictured; and if that being is the symbolic representation of a natural force, which is what all the gods are intended to be, that force will find a channel of manifestation through the form thus built up; the mental image held in the imagination of each participant in the ceremony will suddenly appear to each one to become alive and objective, and they will feel the inrush of the power that has been invoked.

When this process has been repeated regularly over considerable periods, the images that have been built up remain on the astral in exactly the same way that a habit-track is formed in the mind by the repeated performance of the same action. In this form the natural force remains permanently concentrated. Consequently subsequent worshippers need be at no great pains to formulate the simulacrum; they have only to think of the god and they feel his power. It is in this way that all anthropomorphic representations of the God-head have been built up. If we think for a moment we shall see that the Holy Ghost is neither a flame nor a dove; neither is the maternal earth-aspect of Nature either Isis or Ceres or the Virgin Mary. These are the forms under which the human mind contrives to apprehend these things; the lower and less evolved the mind, the grosser the form.

Those who have a knowledge of the little understood aspects of the human mind, whether Egyptian priest, Eleusinian hierophant, or modern occultist, make use of their knowledge of this rarer kind of psychology to create conditions in which the individual human mind shall be able to transcend itself and break through its limitations into a wider air.

4.

The Psychology of Ritual

At the Reformation the men who made the Anglican ritual did not understand the psychological signficance of the Roman ceremonial. They saw it in its degradation as an empty channel, and they broke up the conduit because it was dry. Let us be wiser in our generation, and instead of breaking up the conduit, connect it up with the well-head

There is a spiritual reality behind the forms of organized religion, and it is that reality alone which gives them their value. They are not intended to be a discipline to train the soul, nor even to be a means of pleasing God, but are designed to enable the Light of the Spirit to be brought to a focus in consciousness. If we understand the psychology of ritual we shall neither be in bondage to superstition nor in rebellion against empty forms. We shall realize that a form is the channel for a force, but it is not only the material substance used in a sacrament which is the physical channel for a force, but also the vivid pictorial image created in the mind of the worshipper by its ritual use.

It is to the power behind the symbol that we must look when we seek for the validity of the Church's forms. The outward and visible sign, be it cup or cross, is but the focusing point of attention which enables the worshipper to come into psychic touch with the form of spiritual force which is the animating life of that symbol. We must learn to look to psychology, not to history, for an explanation of the significance of the Church's symbols and rituals. What is commemorated is not a mundane act, but a spiritual reaction, and it is only as we ourselves make that inner reaction that we share in the efficacy of the act which was its prototype. The crucifixion of Our Lord at the hands of Roman authority was but the shadow thrown on the material plane by the struggle that was going on in the spiritual world. It was not the spilling of the blood of Jesus of Nazareth that redeemed mankind, but the outpouring of spiritual power from the mind of Jesus the Christ.

The symbolism which commemorates His death causes us to

concentrate our attention on the Sacrifice of the Cross and the work it accomplished for mankind. The racial subconsciousness of Christian peoples is profoundly imbued with that ideal, and when we contemplate the symbol universally associated with it, we waken the subconscious train of ideas which rouses deep racial memories. The ritual which causes a congregation to concentrate its attention is making use of the group mind. It is well known that the group mind, under the influence of rage or fear, is capable of panics and lynchings of which the individual members composing that crowd are quite incapable; so it is with the impulses of the spiritual life. A congregation is an organized crowd with its attention riveted by appeals to all five physical senses upon a single focus—the sacrifice of the Mass, and the group emotion thus engendered is able to lift the group mind to heights which the individuals composing that congregation are incapable of achieving unaided.

It must not be thought that such an explanation of the psychological aspect of the power of the Eucharist is intended in any way to detract from the recognition of its Divine aspect; it is solely intended to show the manner in which the spiritual forces operate on the level of mind. If we wish to understand the *modus operandi* of the spiritual forces, we must distinguish between the spiritual and the mental. It is the confounding of the two types of psychology which leads to so much misapprehension.

The power of God has to be embodied in a concrete idea if it is to be apprehended by the untrained human mind. Hence the necessity for the Incarnation, which presented God to man in a form which he could grasp.

So the sacraments of the Church are incarnations or embodyings in form of primary spiritual truths, too abstract to be apprehended by the untutored mind. By means of their pictorial symbolism the mind is enbabled to contemplate that which, unaided, it could never conceive. This contemplation enables it to link itself on with the spiritual potency which performs the work shadowed forth by the priest on the physical plane. Thus linked in thought, the spiritual power pours into the soul and accomplishes its divine work.

There are therefore three aspects to a sacrament—the formless power of God translated from the abstract to the concrete by Our Lord; secondly, the symbolic ritual which reminds us of that particular function of Our Lord's work; and thirdly, the image formed in our imagination. When this last forms in consciousness, the circuit is completed, and Our Lord has put us in touch with God.

5.

The Circuit of Force

It is not easy to convey Eastern thought to Western readers because the dictionary equivalent of the terms employed is very far from being their significance in mystical thought. It is well known to those who have penetrated beyond the Outer Court in these matters that there is a special use of language, a *double entendre*, as it were, which is made use of whenever questions of practical procedure are under discussion, lest the 'once-born' should discover the short cuts to the secret places of the soul. It is both right and necessary that this precaution should be used, and it will be observed in these pages; for these short cuts are effectual psychological devices, and can be made use of by the undedicated as well as the dedicated, and if they are employed by persons with unpurified and undisciplined minds can prove unfortunate for others as well as themselves. I would be the last to deny to an adult the right to burn his own fingers if he so desires, but think it best to withhold from him the means of raising conflagrations in other folk.

Another difficulty in the way of conveying Eastern thought to Western readers lies in the fact that the attitude towards life of East and West is entirely different; this is strikingly illustrated by the sacred buildings in the two hemispheres. In the West, the central emblem commemorates suffering: in the East it commemorates joy. The men and women conditioned to these emblems naturally evaluate the experiences of life differently. As Kipling truly said: 'The wildest dreams of Kew are the facts of Khatmandu, and the crimes of Clapham chaste in Martaban.'

The best approach to Eastern thought is through a classical education. The Greek and the Hindu would have no difficulty in understanding each other; each has the same concept of Nature and the same regard for asceticism as a means to an end and not as an end in itself. Eastern thought, however, has penetrated far more deeply into natural religion than the Greeks had the capacity to do, and the Mysteries of Dionysus and Ceres are but pale shadows of their Eastern prototypes.

It may be not without value in this connection to examine what is known concerning the origin of the Greek Mysteries. It is believed, and for the grounds for this belief the reader may turn to the pages of *Prolegomena to the Study of Greek Religion* by Jane Harrison, that when Greek national religion began to lose its hold on an increasingly enlightened people, an attempt was made, by no means unsuccessfully, to provide a rendering of it acceptable to thinking men by borrowing the method of the Egyptian Mysteries and expressing it in terms of the older, earlier Greek Nature cults that preceded the highly poetized tradition of the bright Olympians. These old Nature cults still lingered in the out of the way parts of Greece, in the islands, and in the mountains, and the Mystery myths show clearly that their originators knew this fact, for in them the god comes down from the mountains or the goddess takes refuge in the island. It must be clearly recognized that these Mystery myths are not by any means primitive material, but very sophisticated material indeed, being the work of scholars and mystics of a highly civilized era seeking in the ancient traditional roots of Greek religion for untapped springs of inspiration. It was exactly as if a modern Englishman sought inspiration from Keltic or Norse folk lore. No doubt the initiates of the Mysteries were regarded as pagans in their own day.

There is another fact, which, though known to specialists along this line of study, is unrealized by the majority of writers on mysticism, and consequently by the majority of their readers. It will no doubt be a surprise to many to learn that Indian initiates believe that the inspiration of their Mysteries came originally from Egypt. The relevant data may be found in the works of Sir John Woodroffe (Arthur Avalon). See, in particular, the extract from Panchkori Bandyapadhyga on p. XXIV of Vol. II of that author's *Principles of Tantra*.

It follows then, that those who have been initiated in the Western Esoteric Tradition, and have taken those grades that draw their inspiration from Greece and Egypt in addition to the better-known alchemical grades, will have no difficulty in understanding much in Eastern thought that is obscure, or even obscene to the ordinary student.

The practical applications of such teachings, valuable as they could be as a corrective to our insularity, are, however, far from easy to attain. It is frequently said that Yoga as taught in the East is impractical in the West because the Western conditions of life are utterly unsuited to it, and the Western attitude utterly unsympathetic. I can only repeat this standard advice yet again. The student should on no account attempt the practical work of advanced Yoga unless he has the necessary conditions of mind, body and estate, for all these three play their part. Practical Yoga should not be done in any makeshift manner, but with proper care and attention to all the material conditions that are necessary for its achievement. If these are not available, it is inadvisable to make the attempt with substitutes. Among these necessities are the necessary number of properly trained persons in a properly equipped and prepared place that is secure from profanation. Again I emphasize that makeshifts are worse than useless. If you do Yoga at all, do it under proper conditions or leave it alone.

But despite these provisos and warnings, I think it worthwhile to write on the subject of Yoga because I feel that my training in the ancient Mysteries of the West has given me an insight into it that the average Christian does not possess. There have been a great many books written on the subject, their writers all frankly recognizing that Yoga in its original form is unsuited to the West, and one and all trying to present an adaptation of it that should be suitable; but one and all, so far as my experience goes, have thrown away the baby with the bath-water, and presented a version of that ancient science which is like a version of Hamlet edited by a rationalist who removed all reference to the supernatural. The result does not make sense.

The fact, however, remains that Yoga as it stands does not suit the West, and that if the mountain cannot go to Mahomet, Mahomet will have to go to the mountain if he wants to enjoy the delights of a high altitude. Our Western culture has bestowed many benefits in the way of physical sanitation, but the same cannot always be said of it in regard to mental sanitation, and a modification of its attitude is due, and overdue, as the psychoanalysts have long been pointing out.

In earlier writings I have tried to show the practical implictions of the doctrine of Manifestation by means of the Pairs of Opposites, which is one of the most fundamental and far-reaching tenets of the esoteric tradition. Much of what I have had to say is so profoundly esoteric and so immediately practical that I have been obliged to adhere to the ancient method of myth and metaphor. These things are not for the profane, who would either misunderstand them or abuse them. Those who have eyes to see can read between the lines.

In this present context I will try to sum up the principles involved and bring the whole concept to a single focus; yet even so, such is its inherent nature, as in fact the nature of all manifestation, that my argument must needs move in a circuit, returning whence it started for its final explanation and application.

Manifestation takes place when the One divides into Two that act and react on each other. Manifestation ends when Multiplicity is resolved or absorbed back into Unity. The transition from plane to plane of manifestation takes place in the same manner. In order that any thing or factor shall be brought down from a higher to a lower plane, it is necessary to analyse it into the contradictory factors that are held in equilibrium in its nature. To do this, one imagines the opposite extremes of which it is capable and expresses them separately while retaining in consciousness their essential unity when in equilibrium.

Equally, if it is desired to raise any factor from a lower to a higher plane, one conceives its opposite and reconciles the pair in imagination and realization.

Any pair of factors, divided for the sake of manifestation, act and react upon each other, alternately struggling to unite and, in the act of uniting, exchanging magnetism, and then, their magnetism having been exchanged, repelling each other and striving to draw apart, thus re-establishing their separate individuality; then, this established and a fresh charge of magnetism having been generated, once again they yearn towards each other in order to exchange magnetism, the more potent giving off, and the less potent receiving, the charge. It must never be forgotten in this respect that relative potency is not a fixed thing, depending on mechanism or form, but a variable thing, depending upon voltage or vitality. Moreover, the charge passes backwards and forwards as an alternating current, never with a permanent one-way flow.

These are fundamentals of the concept, and they have their application to every aspect of existence. Ignorance of them, and our inveterate tendency to try and maintain the status quo whenever and wherever it is established, causes endless sterility, as needless as it is destructive and wasteful, and whose cause is utterly unsuspected.

An illustration will serve to show the far-reachng ramifications of the influence of this principle. Apply those concepts to the relationship of initiator and candidate, of leader and follower, of man and woman; then, having so applied them, re-read these pages and see if you can then see what is written between the lines.

But not only is there a flow of magnetism between the Pairs of Opposites, but there is a circulation of force between parts and the whole. Man is a perfect Microcosm of the Macrocosm; none other creature, so it is taught, shares this development. To the angels, the lower aspects are lacking; to the Elementals, the higher. In consequence of his manifold nature, man is in magnetic relationship with the cosmos as a whole, not merely with a limited or selected presentation of it. There is a flow and return between every aspect of our beings and characters and the corresponding aspect in the cosmos. Just as the chemical elements in our dense body are derived from and returned to the general fund of matter, so by the processes of metabolism, the psychic factors in our subtler bodies are neither static nor exclusive, but are maintained by a perpetual flow and return like a hot water circuit which flows from boiler to storage tank and back again by virtue of its own physical properties. If we are for any reason cut off from this free flow of natural force, some aspect of our nature atrophies and dies. Or if the flow is checked without being blocked, some aspect suffers starvation. There is a characteristic deadness when this occurs, readily recognizable in all the relations of life when once its nature is realized. If the initiator is not in contact with spiritual forces, he cannot pass them on to the candidate and so 'fails to initiate.' If the candidate brings no real depth of feeling to his initiation, he gives out no magnetism; and as magnetism can only be poured into a person who is giving it out—a little understood, but far-reaching truth—that candidate receives no down-pouring of power and the initiation is ineffective. If a leader has not great principles to guide him but is a mere opportunist, his inspiration to his followers will consist in no more than a hope for a share of the spoils. If a man and a woman are not each in touch with Nature, they will have little to give each other that is of any vital value and so will soon part—on the inner planes, even if convention holds them together on the outer plane.

The operation of magnetic interchange in all its aspects can be cultivated and developed. In its subjective aspect it is developed by certain Hatha Yoga practices, which, though definitely dangerous if done incorrectly, are very valuable if done correctly. Without this development of the subjective magnetism and the acquirement of skill in its direction and control, it is impossible to operate either safely or satisfactorily the contacts with the corresponding reservoirs of magnetic force in the cosmos; but once some degree of development and skill has been attained, it is a waste of time to persevere with exclusively subjective methods.

Contacts with cosmic forces, however, are not things to be made at random, any more than contact with a lightning flash; therefore formulae are used to enable the mind first to contact and secondly to control the chosen cosmic force. These formulae can, in the case of experienced operators, thoroughly skilled in the art, be purely mental and consist of images in the imagination representative of the force in question. But only very highly developed people can obtain results by purely mental means, and for less developed people, the co-operation of others in group working is necessary. Solitary working soon becomes arid, wearisome, and unproductive of results, as every student of occultism can testify.

Nevertheless, unless there is solitary working, the operator becomes de-magnetized. Consequently we must accustom ourselves to the idea of a perpetual change of state, and alternation between subjective solitary working and objective group working. Not otherwise can we hope to maintain the sense of zest which tells us that the forces are flowing freely.

These things are the secret not only of magical power but of life itself in all its relationships. They are things of which even the most enlightened exoteric thought is entirely ignorant, and they are the real keys to practical occult work. They are the Lost Secrets of the Mysteries, secrets which were lost when an ascetic religion, though a valuable corrective to excess, destroyed the polarizing opposite truth which alone could maintain it in equilibrium. It is the great fault of our ethic that it is incapable of realizing that one can have too much of a good thing.

When, in order to concentrate exclusively on God, we cut ourselves off from nature, we destroy our own roots. There must be in us a circuit between heaven and earth, not a one-way flow, draining us of all vitality. It is not enough that we draw up the Kundalini from the base of the spine; we must also draw down the divine light through the Thousand-Petalled Lotus. Equally, it is not enough for our mental health and spiritual development that we draw down the Divine Light, we must also draw up the earth forces. Only too often mental health is sacrificed to spiritual development through ignorance of, or denial of, this fact. Nature is God made manifest, and we blaspheme Her at our peril.

6.

The Three Kinds of Reality

Unless we realize the difference between the Cosmos and the Universe, we shall never achieve a true understanding of esoteric philosophy. This point is an exceedingly important one, for it marks the distinction between those who know how to interpret the symbol systems and those who do not.

The concept is not an easy one to grasp, but we will try to convey it as simply as possible, for many important practical points arise out of it.

For all practical purposes our solar system is a closed unit. The influences received by it from the other heavenly bodies change, if they change at all, in such vast cycles of time, that we are justified in considering them as constant so far as we are concerned. This solar system arose from a nebula, the planets being thrown off by the sun, and in their turn throwing off their attendant moons. We may therefore say, as regards our universe, 'In the beginning there was a nebula.'

But when we have said that, we have not disposed of the problem. Whence came the original nebula? That it was condensed out of the diffused matter of space, may be the answer to that question. But still we have not got to the beginning. Whence did the matter of space, whatever that may be, derive the inherent characteristics which came out in the process of its evolution? In fact, the very word evolution implies involution. Nothing can be unfolded which was not previously infolded. There must have been a phase of existence which preceded the unfolding of evolution, for evolution is not a continuous creation of something out of nothing, but a coming into manifestation of latencies.

We solve this problem, for the purposes of any reasoning we may want to do, by positing the Great Unmanifest, the Root of All Being, which is really the metaphysical equivalent of X, the unknown quantity. In algebra, X enables calculations to be made with known quantities, but at the end we are none the wiser concerning its own nature than we were when we started. In metaphysics whatever we do not understand, we refer to this X, which is not only the Great Unmanifest, but also the Great Unknown.

The Unknown, however, is a relative term, and esotericists, or for the matter of that, evolutionists also, would not agree with Herbert Spencer that the Great Unknown is also the Great Unknowable. With the extension of human consciousness, either in the course of evolutionary development or by intensive methods, a great deal can become known which was hitherto unknown. In fact a great deal is known to the scientist, the philosopher, the metaphysician, that is a part of the Great Unknown so far as the average man is conccerned; and much is known to the average man which is also part of the Great Unknown to a young child.

The Great Unknown, therefore, is not a thing in itself, but rather a relationship that exists, or perhaps more accurately, does not exist, between the Self and certain aspects of the Not-self.

The Great Unmanifest cannot be the Great Non-Existent. The Non-Existent just *isn't*, and that is all there is to be said about it. But the Great Unmanifest very much *is*, and to call it the Root of All Being is a very good description. It is only unmanifest so far as we are concerned, because we have not got, at our present state of evolution at any rate, any faculties or sense by means of which we are able to contact it. If an extension of consciousness takes place, however, by means of which we become conscious of an aspect of the Root of All Being which had hitherto been unperceived by us, then for us it is no longer Unmanifest, but has become Manifest.

Might we say, then, that manifestation takes place by means of realization? The actualities, which are the underlying noumenal essences of all that exists, never become manifest in that they become objects of sensory experience. But are our apprehensions limited to sensory experience? The psychologist says, yes. The esotericist says, no. No sensory experiences enabled Darwin to apprehend the law of evolution. His five senses may have enabled him to observe the innumerable phenomena on which his ultimate deduction was based, but it was a faculty quite distinct from sensory consciousness by means of which he finally grasped the nature of the underlying cohesion between the innumerable separate units which had passed under his observation in the course of his researches.

Is a formula which resumes a number of objective facts any less a reality than the facts themselves? Does its reality consist in the marks which as figures and letters represent it upon paper? Is it not a thing in itself upon its own plane? We need to disabuse our minds of the idea that only dense matter is real. There are many forms of energy which are not physical. Behind the physical reality there is a psychic reality, and behind the psychic reality there is spiritual reality. To think in terms of matter only is a bad mental habit and gives a totally false outlook upon existence.

The psychic reality we may define by saying that it consists of the sum-total of the realizations, however, dim, that consciousness, however rudimentary, has achieved. Of the spiritual reality, we had best limit ourselves to saying that it consists of the as yet unapprehended Great Unmanifest, and that in it is the Root of All Being.

And even when a psychic reality is formed through realization, the spiritual reality is not done away with, but remains as the underlying essence which gives validity to the whole. For there may be psychic realizations which are not realities, but unrealities, because inadequate or inaccurate, and in them we may look for the root of Positive Evil.

It may well be asked, what practical consequences can there be for us in the work-a-day world as consequence of these fine-spun metaphysical subtleties? When we are bearing the burden and heat of the day, what does it matter to us whether there is a psychic reality as distinguished from the thing-in-itself, the spiritual reality? And would it ease our burden did we know?

It is upon such considerations as these that the whole structure of the practical application of mind-power rests; it is in the field of psychic reality that the reasonings and affirmations of Christian Science and the New Thought movement in general find their scope and derive their power. It is in the field of psychic reality that the adept and the magician work by means of the trained mind, for the plane of psychic reality is susceptible to mental manipulation.

The Inhabitants of the Unseen

Whoever contacts the invisible world, whether by means of his own psychism or by employing the psychism of another as a channel of evocation, has need of some system of classification in order that he may be able to understand the varied phenomena with which he will meet. Not all of them are due to the spirits of the departed; there are other denizens of the invisible world than those who have once had human form. Nor are all the phenomena due to the subconscious mind entirely subjective. Confusion arises when that which should be assigned to one division is allocated to another. It can be clearly shown that the explanation which is offered does not account for the facts. Nevertheless, the facts are not disposed of by showing the explanation to be fallacious.

A correct classification would yield an explanation which can stand up to any impartial investigation and be justified of its wisdom.

The classification which it is proposed to employ in these pages is drawn largely from the traditional occult sources, and it is believed that it will throw light on certain experiences met with by psychic research workers. It is offered in a spirit of co-operation, as independent testimony to a common experience.

I. The Souls of the Departed

Of all the inhabitants of the invisible worlds, the ones with which it is easiest for us to get into touch are the souls of human beings who have shed their outer garment of flesh, either temporarily or permanently. Anyone who is familiar with spiritualistic or esoteric thought soon becomes habituated to the idea that a man is not changed by death. The personality remains, it is only the body that is gone.

The esotericist, in his concept of the nature of departed souls, distinguishes between those who are going through the inter-natal phase, that is to say, who are living in the non-physical worlds between incarnations, and those who will not incarnate again. There is a great difference in capacity and outlook between these two types of souls, and many of the issues at present outstanding between spiritualism and occultism are undoubtedly due to a failure to recognize this fact.

The occultist does not maintain that existence is an eternal sequence of birth and death, but that at a certain phase of evolution the soul enters upon a series of material lives, and through the development made during these lives, it finally outgrows the mundane phase of evolution, becoming more and more spiritualized towards the end of this period, until finally it wins its freedom from matter and reincarnates no more, continuing its existence as a disembodied spirit with a human mind. Mentality, the occultist maintains, can only be obtained through incarnation in human form. Those beings who have not undergone this experience have not got mentality as we understand it, with certain exceptions which we will consider later.

For the most part, it is the souls of the living dead who are contacted in the seance-room. Liberated souls go on to their own place and are not so easily reached. Only those return within range of the earth-sphere who have some business there. The discussion of this point would open up a vast field of interest which we cannot deal with at the moment. It must suffice to say that, as is well known to all workers in psychic research, there are souls of a higher type than those commonly encountered, who are concerned with the evolution of humanity and the training of those who are willing to co-operate with them in their work.

We may say, then, that the souls of the departed may be divided into three types: the souls of the living dead, who will return again to the earth-life; liberated souls who have outgrown earth-life and have gone on to another sphere of existence; and the liberated souls who, having gone on, return again to the earth-sphere because they have work to do therein. A recognition of these three types of departed souls will serve to explain many of the discrepancies we encounter between the statements of spiritualists and occultists. The occultist aims chiefly at getting into touch with the liberated souls for the purposes of specific work in which both he and they are concerned; for the most part, he leaves the souls of the living dead severely alone. Personally, I am of the opinion that he is mistaken in so doing. It is quite true that they can be of little assistance to him in his chosen work, but the normal companionship of the living with the dead robs death of most of its terrors and is steadily building a bridge between those who remain and those who have passed over. The occultist should certainly not invite the co-operation of the living dead as he would that of the liberated souls, for they have their own work to do; nor can he place as much reliance on their knowledge and insight as on that of those who are freed from the wheel of birth and death; neither has he any right to try to use them as he would Elemental spirits in the course of his experiments. Admitting these qualifications, however, there seems no reason why the occultist should not share in the interchange of amenities which is continually taking place across the borderline. After all, death is one of the processes of life, and the dead are very much alive and quite normal.

II. Projections of the Living

The appearance of a simulacrum of a human being at the point of death is exceedingly common, and innumerable well-attested instances exist of its occurrence. It is not so well known, however, that it is possible for the simulacrum, or astro-etheric form, to be projected voluntarily by the trained occultist. Such projections, in proportion to the hosts of disembodied souls encountered when the threshold is crossed, are exceedingly rare; nevertheless they occur, and may be met with, therefore they must be included in any classification which aims at being comprehensive. Usually such a projected soul appears to be entirely preoccupied with its own affairs and in a state of absorption which causes it to appear to ignore its surroundings. As a matter of fact, it most frequently happens that the disembodied spirit has its work cut out to maintain consciousness at all on the higher planes, and its self-absorption is that of the beginner on a bicycle. Occasionally communication may be established between such a projected etheric body and a group of experimenters, and very interesting results are obtained; but unless there is sufficient materialization to render the simulacrum visible to the non-psychic, the experiment will partake rather of the nature of telepathy grafted upon mediumship than of a true projection of the astro-etheric form.

Such visitants are neither angels nor devils but 'human, all too human.'

III. The Angelic Hierarchies

The average Protestant has a very dim notion concerning the angelic hierarchies, the great hosts of beings of another evolution than ours, though children of the same Heavenly Father. The Qabalah, however, is explicit on this point, and classifies them into ten archangels and ten orders of angelic beings. Buddhist, Hindu and Mohammedan theology are equally explicit. We may therefore reckon that in this agreement of witnesses there is surety of testimony, and it may serve our purpose best to take for our guide that system from which Christianity took its rise—mystic Judaism.

We will not go into the elaborate classifications employed by the Jewish rabbis, which have their importance for purposes of magic but are not germane to our present issue. It is enough that we realize that there are divinely created beings of varying degrees of greatness, from the mighty archangel whom St John the Divine saw standing in the sun, down to the nameless heavenly messengers who have from time to time visited mankind.

Beyond the spheres to which are assigned the disembodied spirits of humanity dwell these heavenly beings, and in some high ranges of spiritual light the psychic or medium sometimes touches them. In the Vale Owen scripts there is much concerning them that is of great interest.

It is said by the rabbis that these beings are perfect, each after their kind; but they do not evolve, and it is noticeable that they are non-intellectual. One might almost call them divine robots, each strictly conditioned by its own nature perfectly to fulfil the office for which it was created; free from all struggle and inner conflict, but changeless, and therefore unevolving.

No angel, it is held, ever goes outside his own sphere of activity. The angel who has 'healing in his wings' cannot bestow vision, nor the bestower of visions serve as the strong guard against the powers of darkness.

Esotericists make a fundamental distinction between angels and the souls of men. They say that the Divine Sparks, which are the nuclei of the souls of men, proceed from the noumenal cosmos, from the same plane whereon the Solar Logos has His being. They are therefore, of the same innermost nature as the Godhead. Angels, on the other hand, are created by the Solar Logos as the first of His created beings. They neither fall into generation, nor rise by regeneration, but remain in changeless but unevolving perfection till the end of the epoch.

The functions of the angels are diverse, and cannot be entered upon here in detail. They are, each according to his office and rank, God's messengers in things of the spirit, but they have no direct contact with dense matter. That office is performed by another order of beings altogether, the Elementals, who differ in origin and inmost nature from both angels and men.

IV. Elementals

Much confusion of thought exists concerning the orders of beings known as Elementals. They are sometimes confused with the spirits of men. Undoubtedly many happenings attributed to spirits are to be assigned to the activities of these other orders of beings. Again, they are not to be confused with the evil demons, or, to give them the Qabalistic name, the Qliphoth.

Elementals are the thought-forms generated by co-ordinated systems of reactions that have become stereotyped by constant and unchanging repetition. Some explanation is necessary to make this concept clear, and we shall understand it best if we survey the means by which elementals come into being.

Each epoch of evolution is constituted by the outgoing and return of a live-wave of living souls. These are referred to in esoteric terminology as the Lords of Flame, of Form, and of Mind. The present evolution will become the Lords of Humanity. Each life-wave develops its characteristic contribution to evolution. When the Divine Sparks which constituted the nuclei of the evolving souls of each evolution are withdrawn back up the planes and reabsorbed into the Kingdom of God, their work remains behind them in that which they have builded, whether it be the chemical elements evolved by the Lords of Flame, or the reactions of consciousness evolved by the Lords of Mind.

Humanity, it is held, is evolving the power of co-ordinated

consciousness, and the Lords of Humanity therefore hold the same relationship to the Lords of Mind that the Lords of Flame hold to the Lords of Form. These beings, however, of the three earlier life-waves, have passed out of range of the life of our earth, each group to its appropriate plane, and the Lords of Humanity are still absorbed in the task of building, and are not yet, save those few who have become Masters, escaped from the bondage of the material in which they work. Consequently, it is but rarely that any psychic save the higher grades of adept ever contacts any of these beings.

They have left behind them, however, as has already been noted, the forms which they built up in the course of their evolution. These forms, as psychics teach, actually consist of co-ordinated systems of magnetic stresses. Whenever any movement takes place an electric current is set up, and if the series of co-ordinated movements is repeated many times, these currents tend to make adjustments among themselves and become co-ordinated on their own account, quite independently of the physical forms whose activities gave rise to them. It is out of these co-ordinators that the Elementals are evolved.

We cannot go more deeply into this most interesting and intricate subject in the present pages. It is a matter for a separate study. Enough has been said, however, to indicate that although the ultimate product of the evolution of the angelic, the human, and the Elemental kingdom is to produce consciousness and intelligence, the origin of the three types of beings is entirely different, and so also is their destiny.

The Divine Sparks are the emanations of the Great Unmanifest, Ain Soph Aur, in the terminology of the Qabalists; the angels are the creations of the Solar Logos, and the Elementals are 'the creations of the created', that is to say, they are developed out of the activities of the material universe.

Of the Elementals thus evolved there are many types. Firstly, the four great divisions of the Elemental spirits of Earth, Air, Fire and Water, known respectively to the Alchemists as Gnomes, Sylphs, Salamanders, and Undines. These really represent four types of activity arising out of four types of relationship. In solids (the Element of earth), the molecules adhere together. In liquids (the Element of water), the molecules are free-moving. In gases (the Element of air), they repel each other and therefore diffuse to their uttermost limits. And in the fire the essential property of its activity is to change plane, or transmute. The four kingdoms of primary Elementals, under their angelic kings represent the co-ordinated, purposive, and intelligent action of these four properties of matter—the mind-side of the material phenomena, to be precise.

This fact is well known to occultists, and they employ the mind-side of matter in their magical work. Consequently many of these Elemental systems of reactions have, as it were, been domesticated by adepts. Elementals thus domesticated become imbued with consciousness of a human type. These developed (or initiated) Elementals are sometimes met with by psychics.

We are now trenching upon some of the most secret aspects of occultism, and not a great deal can be said; and even if it were said little of it would be understood save by those who were already well versed in esoteric science.

7.

Non-humans

By this term in this section we mean in a general way every sort of sentient intelligence which is not at the time incarnated in a human body—this includes those discarnate spirits who speak through mediums and those we call Masters or Inner Plane Adepti, not sharing in our human life, though human spirits, but we reckon them as non-human for purposes of classification. We will take the contact with beings who are not in physical bodies. We read a great deal about these contacts in medieval literature, so too have the ancients a lot to say, and today among the primitive tribes of the East and of the New World. Also there is a good deal about it in certain sections of our own folklore, especially among the Celts. The average Anglo-Saxon is content with one non-human only, and that is the Devil. So then we are dealing with a considerable body of testimony to the contact between human beings and non-humans, and there is no smoke without fire. So we have to consider. Are there such things? Is communication possible, and if so, is it advisable under any conditions or certain conditions?

Taking the broad question of other phases of evolution, there is no reason why there should not be other forms of existence than dense physical matter. To the untrained person, nothing is real but the material things he can bump into and fall over. But anyone with any experience in scientific work knows that there are unseen forces of existence on the level next removed from dense matter which we can get at with absolute certainty. Why should there not be others just a little further on? Are we to limit ourselves to that we can see, or are we to say that there are more things in heaven and earth than are dreamt of in our philosophy?

We will take this for granted now to save our time, and go on to consider the nature of the non-humans. Esoteric Science teaches us that there are other lines of evolution as well as our own. Just as light and sound take up no space in our air, so these beings do not occupy space, have not got weight or mass, they interpenetrate matter and you might walk through one, as through a ghost. They are different modes of consciousness from ours. We might see a musician in raptures, in a state of rapture at what might sound to us a mere din, because his trained ear distinguishes the sounds. So there are these other modes of existence different from ours, and they interpenetrate ours. We contact these other modes of life only under three conditions. We have to begin to perceive in a different way; then we find that we are meeting with beings of a kind that we did not know existed, and it is a surprising experience for both. Secondly, we may come into contact with these other beings if there is someone about who is a materializing medium and who can exude ectoplasm. Thirdly, occultists who go in for such forms of work, by magical operations can invoke beings of other forms of existence into materialization. So then we see there are conditions by which we can contact them, but it is a process out of the normal for both parties. When a human being raises consciousness to the subtle planes, he is, as it were, a ghost to the inhabitants of that plane. Therefore when we do, we get a sense of danger, of things inimical to us; the reason being that these beings are afraid of us and on the defensive. It is different in the case of the initiated occultist, who goes out into the unseen with 'letters of introduction', and there is a fraternal relationship. Then the consciousness of the adept moves out along well-known tracks with his credentials, and he no longer finds these planes antagonistic, he knows how to behave, and it is an entirely different matter. But these journeys are not things to be undertaken haphazardly by anyone. We can give much offence to the beings of another plane and be pushed back forcibly. The question of communication between the two planes resolves itself into the change of the levels of consciousness on our side, or the assembling of a substantial form on the other side, and in both it is essential that both shall know what they are about and observe certain precautions.

And now what manner of beings are they who are thus contacted? First, there are living dead, those whom the Spiritualists usually contact when they reach the unseen. The Spiritualist movement was brought into being about the same time as the modern Occult movement and Christian Science. Four big movements moved off in the last quarter of the last century—Spiritualism; Christian Science and its allies, New Thought, etc.; the Theosophical Society under Blavatsky; and a general stirring and movement of life in the Western Esoteric Tradition itself, which is much less known. Each of these had its own work to do. The Spiritualists had for their work association with the human spirits of the departed

who were still within the earth's sphere. They never did much outside
that. Just as the occultist working on his contacts up and down a given
ray comes in touch with beings of his ray, so the Spiritualists work, and
so their experience is limited. These beings are human Personalities.
Most of you know that the human Personality endures for a while after
the death of the body, going through a purgatorial experience, from there
to a lower heaven to rest in a pleasant dream, then to the Second Death,
the death of the Personality of this incarnation, including the lower mind,
which is disintegrated; from this the Higher Self is set free and passes
some time in the higher heaven before reincarnating. The type that the
Spiritualist meets with are beings in the lower heaven; I do not think
there is any sign of beings who are functioning in the Individuality. It
is the function of the Spiritualist movement to work with beings on these
levels because its work was to break down the barrier between the living
and the dead. The occultist, on the other hand, is forbidden by his
conditions to have any dealings with the living dead. He opens up his
contact with those of the human kind who have passed beyond the
reincarnating phase of evolution, and also with some other different forms
of existence which are very interesting. So then the occultist finds that
when he is able to function in his higher consciousness, he is coming
across beings of quite different kinds from himself. These are classified.
We may take them as being the Elemental beings. They are quite different
in kind from humanity. They have no Divine Spark; they will be
disintegrated at the end of this evolution and cease to exist, unless they
can develop within themselves a spiritual nature. These beings come
into existence thus—Wherever you get a series of constantly co-ordinating
actions and reactions, you get what we call 'tracks in space', which remain
after the activities which gave rise to them have ceased. We can compare
them to the swirling of the water in a stirred-up basin: after the stirring
has ceased the swirls in the water continue for some time. These
throughout nature are the basis of any beings and on this basis develop
the possibilities of response to environment and memory. Thus we
gradually get the difficult concept of the building up of consciousness
out of natural phenomena. The Building Spirits, who thus operated in
the first place the great natural phenomena when they were being created,
are Angelic Beings. They withdraw up the planes, and leave the Elementary
consciousnesses to carry on with the stereotyped mode of reaction. These
remain and develop, and we call them 'the creations of the created'—
these lives called into existence not by God, but by God's creatures, who
have no power to endow them with immortal life. Whenever you get

a system in nature which reacts as a unit, a mountain, a dell, a wood, you have the same system of co-ordinated stresses in the background, and thus come the little nature spirits, or Devas, or gods of localities, which our ancestors worshipped. The same idea is at the back of different species of animals. If you have any knowledge of biology you will know there are very simple beings, uni-cellular, and the generalized consciousness of these may not have a single life under its control, but many. There are certain periods in its existence when there is only a green patch on some damp surface and this breaks up into innumerable little things; these live for a time in a free-swimming form, then they all gather together and form a large homogenous mass, called plasmodeum. What becomes of the consciousness as a unit in its free-moving form? Or take bees; the hive is the unit there, and not the bee. The unit might be called the bee-angel. We get these different curious units of consciousness evolved. Next, what is the logical outcome? Higher, more developed modes of nature forces. There is a very curious occult doctrine, that these beings, becoming more and more developed and coming more to resemble the types of consciousness with which we are familiar, become conscious that they are lost souls unless they can develop a spiritual nature. They seek as initiators those who have got a spiritual nature; the initiated man is the initiator of the Elemental being: Humans take them as pupils and help them to develop their 'sparks' of individual consciousness. In return for this service the Elemental beings perform services for the magician. We read of these as familiar spirits. The writers on these matters were usually the priests, and being charged by the Inquisition to enquire into it, were usually a little prejudiced. But there is a certain relationship between people who understand the inner planes and beings of another order. And there is also an involutionary relationship, very often, between those people who are naturally psychic without training and quite spontaneously come into touch with other beings. The effect of this is seldom wholesome. It has the effect of unbalancing them. It is a too intensely stimulating contact. Elementals are of a pure type, composed of one Element only, whichever that may be, whereas a human being is a mixture of all. So they are too potent a stimulus to that one Element in our own being, which is very apt to throw a human being off his balance, lure him to follow it and abandon his human ways. He is 'taken by the fairies', or what we should call a pathology. You can see the thought control withdrawing from the physical vehicle. They hear the call of the fairies, and only an empty shell remains, insane. When the magician invokes a spirit to individual appearance, he puts himself into a circle and draws a triangle outside it and causes the spirit to manifest in this; then he will do the banishing ritual and return it whence it came, to its own sphere. But he usually does this only for research work, or to help a pathology. We must draw the distinction between the serious research worker and the person who is out for experimenting. Nothing but harm is likely to result in this latter way.

What other forms of creatures are there? I have mentioned the Angelic Beings, the great Archons, the building spirits who built up the planes of nature in the time of other evolutions. There are all manner of very lofty spiritual beings whose mode of manifestation is in nature. They are classified in different ways. We talk about the heathen who worship many gods, but in every religion there is always the Being behind the gods, the Father of the gods, the Oversoul, a very abstract conception of a Being. The 'gods' of any system are these natural forces, called the Archangels and Angels in the Hebrew system which we ourselves use. The spiritual beings have never had a material incarnation, have never descended into matter. The old tradition is that the choice was offered to the spirits whether they would remain on the inner planes, neither ascending nor descending, or descend to the depths of matter in order to rise higher than they had started from; and one lot chose one line, led by Adam, or rather Eve, and others chose the other. So the angelic hosts are our kin and if you go far enough back you find a time when men and angels were of one company. Thus it is possible under certain conditions to contact these angelic beings, but in most cases we do not contact the actual being, who is very vast; we contact his ray, his emanation. If you were sufficiently rich you could engage a great opera singer to come to your house and sing in your drawing-room; but if you had only enough for a wireless set, you could hear him on the air. When we invoke the Archangel Raphael we do not expect him to turn up in person, but we do expect to feel his force, his ray. It is the same with the visions of Christ that have been seen, the Vision Beautiful. It is not the actual being, but tuning in on the ray, though it is the same thing for practical purposes. We need to understand these things. We are not dealing with an actual anthropological form, but with modes of consciousness, and some are so different from ours that there is no analogy. We must not think of them all as fairy figures; they are consciousnesses which are quite incomprehensible to us.

In addition to all these, there is an innumerable host of thought-forms, cast off from human consciousness, artificial Elementals deliberately made

by human beings. These last for various lengths of time so that there
is a legion of different types of beings, neither angels nor devils. The
idea that all which is not physical is either divine or evil is not true.
Non-humans are very much like humans, neither perfect nor omniscient,
but evolving. A final point—the beings which the Qabalists call the
Qliphoth. These are demoniacal, dwelling in the Kingdom of Unbalanced
Force, which came into existence before equilibrium was established;
different types of inharmony, reinforced by the mass of evil thoughts
ever since. When you touch the Unseen, you are unlikely to touch the
divine beings of any sphere without also touching the Qliphoth of that
sphere. If you contact a Sephira you touch its unbalanced side also. You
dare not open up a higher contact with any of these spheres unless you
are able to hold down the lower. This is a great truth of the spiritual
life. The initiated adept knows this. He always aims at the equilibration
of these great forces. At the last, all the kingdoms of the earth and below
the earth shall be redeemed. Our Lord went to preach to the spirits in
prison to redeem them. They are simply misplaced force, which when
returned to its proper place, ceases to be evil. The adept may not curse
the devils; he must replace them to equilibrate them. The adept never
speaks of hell, but of the kingdoms of unbalanced force. The Tree of
Life enables us to travel about on the thirty-two paths, which are distinct
and well-trodden ways and the adept moves about among the Elemental
beings with accuracy, and knows where he is; he can maintain his
equilibrium.

What useful purpose does it serve to contact these forces? First, it
is sometimes necessary for the adept to open up these conditions in
order to clear up something that has gone wrong with a soul. He may
have to open a sphere to operate, like a surgeon, to bring into equilibrium
and to return into its own sphere what has gone wrong. Also, he may
operate the forces of a sphere in order to bring the concentrated forces
of that sphere into his own being, so that he may work with it. Thirdly,
it may be he has some special work to do which he can only carry out
this way. In short, to bring harmony, to intensify his own nature, and
possibly for other reasons. This kingdom is of varied nature. The
conditions under which communication can be rightly done are rare;
there should be a distinct turning off and on of the tap; but things can
be effected by these means which are otherwise impossible.

Haphazard communication is more or less of a crime and the
consequences can be disastrous. Then why not keep this knowledge
secret? Because there is so much of it about that it is better, probably,

to see what is going on. If you bump into things in the dark, it is better to have a light to see what is happening and to bring control. These forces exist. They can be dealt with. It is well to know this, as there is already so much knowledge about.

8.

Black Magic

Black magic is not a thing that any normal person would study or pursue for its own sake, but it is hardly possible, and hardly advisable, to study the technical methods of occultism without giving consideration to the pathologies to which they are liable. Such popular attention as occultism receives is for the most part confined to its black aspect; revelations of this aspect can always command the kind of attention that is given to a street accident. Anyone who has any knowledge of occultism, however, is always struck by the fact that the would-be exposers never get their fingers on the real evil. They sense the evil, just as animals sense an abattoir, but they have no realization of the significance of the facts they record, nor any understanding of why the people concerned are doing such things.

The technique of black magic differs in no way from that of white magic; the same principles apply, the same methods are made use of; the same training in concentration is necessary; the difference lies in the attitude of the operator, the symbolism employed, and the powers contacted thereby; just as the same musical education is necessary to the conductor of a symphony orchestra or a jazz band. And even when we say that certain symbols and powers belong to the domain of black magic, we must make reservations, for these symbols may be used, and these powers evoked quite legitimately, just as dangerous risks are taken by surgeons upon occasion. One can safely say, however, that should any of these magical methods be exhibited to an audience, they can be unhesitatingly classified as black, because they cannot fail to arouse the baser instincts of the spectators, who are there for no useful purpose. There are also certain techniques of sex and blood magic which, though they may be harmless enough among primitive peoples, are certainly out of place among civilized ones, and are only resorted to for the sake of a debased sensationalism. To these we must add the deliberate evocation of evil; this is usually only performed for purposes of revenge.

But there are certain types of persons with a natural streak of cruelty in their natures; these readily take to the evocation of evil for vengeful purposes, and having had experience of the results of this operation, develop a liking for it for its own sake and become cruelty addicts for the sake of the thrill it gives. Unless we recognize this peculiar trait in human nature, which is much commoner than is generally realized, and is distinguished by psychologists by the name of sadism, we shall never understand certain aspects of black magic, for it is in sadism that the key to these is to be sought.

The invocation of certain primitive types of natural forces, though not intrinsically black, is an operation that is very liable to go septic, and should only be done by experienced and dedicated operators working under laboratory conditions. It is an important part of the training of every adept, for when cosmic forces are invoked, they always come up in pairs, action and reaction being equal and opposite; but he would never dream of evoking the unbalanced or Qliphotic aspect by itself or for its own sake, that being too risky an operation. For practical purposes, when Elemental forces are handled, they are dealt with in their sublimated forms, Skehmet, the Lion-headed fire-goddess, for instance, being a preferable form to Kali. These crude forms of force, however, have to be understood by the occultist or he will have trouble with them.

Anyone who makes a serious study of occultism has got to understand these things, and people are not to be branded as black because they study them; in fact they would be very superficial students if they did not; but anyone who makes a public exhibition or popular exposition of black magic most certainly stands condemned; for it is not necessary that anyone save specialists should be acquainted with these things, and it is better for the general run of mankind to leave them alone; for to dwell upon them tends to put one in touch with them, and unless one takes the precautions that the initiate takes when dealing with them, one is liable to infection.

One cannot divide magic into white and black by a clear-cut dividing line; there is what may be described as grey magic, which people embark upon out of ignorance or love of sensation. One must therefore recognize the grey variety, of which there is a great deal more in the world than either the white or the black; but we must also say this of it; that while white is white, it is only a question of degree for grey to shade into black. There is one acid test which can be applied to every variety of operation— in white magic the operation is alway designed and carried out with due regard to cosmic law; any operation which takes no account of cosmic

law but goes its own way regardless of what the spiritual principles of
the matter may be, can be classified as grey; and any operation which
deliberately defies cosmic law can be classified as black.

Let us make this clear by examples. Some people, finding the mental
diet of modern life deficient in spiritual vitamins, turn to the inspiration
of the ancient pagan gods. This is not black magic provided one recognizes
that Aphrodite Anadyomene is one thing, and Aphrodite Cotytto is
another. It is, in fact, a very useful corrective medicine for the modern
mind. It is one, moreover, that we take in constant small doses without
knowing it, because so much of art and poetry draws its inspiration
from the classics. This is an operation which narrow-minded persons
might call black magic, but no one with any insight into life or knowledge
of psychology would consider it so.

On the other hand, indiscriminate dabbling in seances, fortune-telling,
psychism, and suchlike is classified as grey under our definition, because
it takes no account of anything save personal desires, and never asks
itself what may be the spiritual quality of what it is doing. No obvious
evil being immediately forthcoming, and in fact a plentiful amount of
specious piousness being very much in evidence—a form of piousness
wherein God is called upon to bless what is being done, but is never
asked whether it is according to His will—it is taken for granted that
what is afoot is a harmless entertainment, or even actively edifying as
tending to rase the mind above materialism, thus reinforcing faith; the
after-effects are far-reaching, and though they may not necessarily involve
moral deterioration in persons of naturally wholesome character—and
we must acquit them of that charge so often brought—they do cause
a marked deterioration in the quality of the mind, and especially of the
capacity for logic and judgment. Any form of promiscuous psychic or
supernormal dabbling is definitely undesirable, in my opinion, and unfits
the person who indulges in it for serious work.

9.

A Magical Body

James Branch Cabell has a story of the dull, ordinary Felix Kennaston who makes for himself an imaginary personality named 'Horvendile' through whom he experiences high adventure. Such play is common with children, but the shades of the prison house close around most of us, and a field of fascinating experience and experiment is lost just when it is becoming fruitful. In the vicarious imaginings of film and novel we find a substitute for the creations of our own imagination that we are too dull or too self-conscious to trust any longer.

When the girders of the mind are unloosed in psychopathic states, the creative imagination produces strange things for our undoing. It may terrify us with phantasms of the primeval past, or turn us into lotus-eaters neglectful of reality. When the nuclear consciousness retains control, the same destroying element in the psyche can be disciplined into creation through art-forms, so sophisticated and stylized that their original content is hardly discernible save when it is working on the traditional material of myth and folklore. Through this connecting link we can trace the relationship between the creative imagination of the artist and the technique of the adept who uses myths as his formulae. Both are working with the same level of the subliminal mind, and each has something of the other in him; perhaps the degree of creativeness in either branch of art or magic depends on the proportion in which the other is present.

There is a technique in the repertoire of the adept by means of which he builds himself just such a vehicle of experience as Cabell made his dreary hero create in the imaginary personality of 'Horvendile'. Equipped with such an instrument formed out of such stuff as dreams are made of we can enter the dream world of the astral plane and act out therein a dramatic representation of our subliminal lives. Whether this be good for mental health or not depends upon the degree of good sense we bring to it. The escape from reality into fantasy may be a dangerous psychological device, but a holiday from reality may have much to recommend it in the shape of compensation and refreshment.

But if the inner planes be indeed the planes of causation for this world of form and matter, the results of such expeditions may be far-reaching, for we may set in motion all manner of subtle influences whose effects will ultimately reach our bourne of time and space in ever-widening circles. Such enterprises are not to be despised, and patient and bold experimentation may yield results well worth the effort and risk—if risk there be. Personally, I think there is little or none for the well-integrated personality that understands the psychology of the proceeding; no more risk, in fact, than is attached to any other work of the creative imagination to which one trusts oneself—the house may fall upon the bad architect, or the bridge collapse under the incompetent engineer, or any other work of human genius blow up and slay its maker if it be in its nature to explode, but we do not for that reason abandon the work of mechanical invention as too risky to be a justifiable field of human endeavour.

So here are some notes on the subject of such experiments, tentative, for the work is in its early stages, but useful perhaps as throwing light on obscure aspects of the human mind, normal as well as abnormal.

I had long been familiar with the method of going forth by night in the Horvendile body, but was unable to practise it successfully until I was given my 'magical name'. The magical name, whether given by the teacher or discovered by oneself, seems to be an important point in the process of the formulation of the Horvendile body; it appears to play the same part as the grain of sand plays in the formation of the pearl. The psychology of the uses of the magical name needs more study than I can give it at the moment without digression. It must suffice to say that its uses are traditional and I have proved its efficacy in practice. Like most people of vivid imagination I am no stranger to the indulgence in flights of fancy wherein I am the centre of romantic adventures in my own person; like most fiction writers I have put something of myself into my characters; but the creation of a magical personality is a different matter, for if it is to be of any value, it must be in every way greater than oneself, and how can the part be more than the whole that gives rise to it?

The problem is apparently solved by going back into the past of our evolutionary history to a period when the intellect had not obliterated the primitive levels of consciousness, and using the mind of today to direct the sublimal activities. It is, in fact, the method of the psychopath reversed, for in his case it is the primitive levels that rise up and flood the conscious mind, usurping the throne of the nucleus of consciousness.

It may be that the use of the magical name has some relationship to the process of going back into a time past and reawakening the mode of consciousness of a phase of development long outgrown. Primitive names are imitative sounds or descriptive phrases, and so the barbarous syllables of the magical names may serve to awaken memories in the far-wandering soul. We cannot unfold in evolution that which was not infolded in involution; we forget that a phase of preparation must precede all manifestation. We possessed powers in the primitive phases of our development which have had to be sacrificed in order to achieve the higher powers of the human mind. If, while retaining these powers, we can recover the lost secrets, we have the means of fashioning a Horvendile consciousness that shall transcend the limits of its creator, for we have added the past to the present, or, if another terminology be preferred, we have extended consciousness into the realms usually occupied by subconsciousness.

In my own experience of the operation, the utterance to myself of my magical name led to the picturing of myself in an idealized form, not differing in type, but upon an altogether grander scale, superhuman, in fact, but recognizable as myself, as a stuatue more than life-size may yet be a good likeness. Once perceived, I could re-picture this idealized version of my body and personality at will, but I could not identify myself with it *unless I uttered my magical name*. Upon my affirming it as my own, identification was immediate. Consciousness transferred itself to the form thus visualized, and I stepped forth into the world of dreams *naked*. Upon that nudity, as of an antique statue, I could, by a simple act of the imagination, put on whatever robes or drapery I desired to symbolize the part I wished to play.

The subconscious level of the mind was built up while humanity was upon the astral plane while coming down the involutionary arc into immersion in matter, and the subconscious mind still retains its astral methods of mentation, which are in terms of emotional values and pictorial images; and it is by obtaining an understanding of the workings of the subconscious mind that we can best appreciate the workings of the elemental consciousness. Equally, it is by recovering access to the subconscious levels of the mind that we become able to function upon the astral plane. It is for this reason that impressions of the astral realms are always greatly confused by the admixture of subjective subconscious elements. The average human subconscious mind in civilized communities is mainly subjective, but the average human subconscious in primitive races is largely objective as well, that is to say, it is conscious of its astral environment; hence the prevalence of magic among primitive peoples, for they are natural magicians. The occultist, in the course of his training, learns to extend the threshold of consciousness once more into the subconscious mind; but whereas in primitive humanity the mentality ended with subconsciousness, in the evolved man, the powers of the operation of the subconscious astral faculties.

Initiation into the astral plane means more, however, than the exploitation of the psychic powers. The astral plane is the plane of control for the great reservoir of etheric energy, and when we obtain the right of entry upon the astral plane, we also obtain access to and control of the etheric sub-planes of the physical plane. It is from these sub-planes that the vital forces of physical organisms are derived, and it is contact with these great natural reservoirs of force which gives the peculiar magnetic quality so noticeable in souls who have the elemental contacts.

The contacts of the Green Ray are also spoken of as the Celtic Initiation, and for this reason the initiations which were worked by the Greeks and the Druids were of the Upper Astral, in contradistinction to the initiations of an earlier epoch, which were initiations of the Lower Astral, as witness the terrible deities of Akkad and Babylon. The Greeks with their art and the Celts with their music and dance were the true initiates of the Green Ray, and the influence of the astral contacts can be clearly seen to this day in the temperament of the Celtic races.

The Green Ray is essentially the ray of the artist, for it is the subconscious or astral mind which is the creative factor in the arts, and according to the proportion of this mentation which prevails is the degree of inspiration. Technique is of the conscious human mind, but the true creative artistic impulse is of the ancient astral mind of the race which lies hidden below the threshold of superimposed consciousness. Without the technique so painfully acquired by the discipline of hand and eye, there can be no manifestation in matter of the creative astral impulse. There are many such, who, having the astral contacts cannot reduce them to the forms of the physical plane. These tend to get drawn off that plane and over into the astral, and we see in them those extremes of the artistic temperament which tend towards mental unbalance.

Equally, there are certain types of insanity, and certain symptoms in several insanities of purely physical origin, which can be explained in the light of our knowledge of the astral realm, for just as there are certain drugs of the hashish variety which artifically open the psychic centres to the perception of the astral, so there are certain toxic conditions of the blood which act in the same way, and this explains many of the hallucinations of the insane, who are really experiencing a pathological psychism, and seeing about them the denizens of the astral, and also their own thought-forms with which their own auras teem. Psychology explains the latter phenomena quite satisfactorily, but it does not understand the former, and has recourse to far-fetched explanations in order to bring it into line with the previous class of phenomena which it is able to account for satisfactorily. The psychology of insanity is able to throw light upon many of the phenomena of psychic experience, and this is said in no derogatory spirit, but because it is the simple truth, for the hallucinations of insanity are a type of astral phenomena which have been worked out in the light of modern science.

Many other aspects await that process for their elucidation; and when science, and especially the sciences that deal with the human personality, both mental and physical, realize the function and nature of the astral influences working in and upon dense matter, a great step will have been taken and a new era of scientific discovery opened up. At the present moment we are hovering upon the eve of this realization, as a drop of water hangs on the lip of a beaker; when the force of gravity overcomes capillary attraction, the flow will commence. When there is a realization of the invisible, imponderable realities, a new era of scientific discovery and therapeutic achievement will open up. It is a lack of this realization which is baffling science at the present moment and rendering abortive such lines of research as the investigation of cancer and the endocrines, both, as the occultist knows, so intimately connected with the astral plane.

We may well ask why any serious student of occultism (and none others are wanted in the Mysteries) should seek the contacts of the Green Ray in the present age, when both the Hermetic and Christian contacts are open to him. The Hermetic student seeks them in order to complete his intiations, so that he may be able to bring the powers down the planes to their final manifestation on the physical plane. Especially is this contact necessary to him if he be also an esoteric therapeutist, for the processes of both disease and repair are intimately associated with astral conditions, which influence consciousness directly and the physical body indirectly through their effect upon the etheric double. The esoteric therapeutist must therefore of necessity have the contacts of the astral plane.

10.

The Occult Field Today

The publication of two very important books on magic, *The Tree of Life* by Israel Rgardie, and *Magick* by the 'Master Therion' (Aleister Crowley), makes it advisable for the Fraternity of the Inner Light to define its position in these matters. It will be obvious to anyone who compares these books with each other and with the method that is explained in my book *The Mystical Qabalah* that the same system is being used in all three. Some explanation is therefore desirable lest anyone be accused of plagiarism, or stealing another person's thunder; or, equally, be regarded as associated with, or representative of, one of the others.

The explanation is quite simple: all three are drawing from the same source, which I have always referred to as the Western Esoteric Tradition. This Tradition was reorganized and made available for English students by the late S. L. MacGregor Mathers, into whose hands came a number of cipher MSS, and who had the occult knowledge necessary for their use. He claimed to have got into touch with the sources whence these MSS emanated, and there is a certain amount of objective evidence in support of this claim; but the whole subject is wrapped in mystery by the extreme secrecy he observed, and by the drastic initiation oaths demanded of all to whom he taught what he had learnt; and even to these he was extremely uncommunicative on many vital points.

But be that as it may; and whether he came by his system as he said he did, or whether he made it up out of his own head, in actual practice it worked as a highly efficient and satisfactory system of practical occultism and a Way of Initiation. The proof of the pudding is in the eating in occult affairs; high-sounding titles and limitless claims, such as certain American organizations have accustomed us to in these matters, carry no weight at all with those who have any knowledge of the subject and its history or any practical experience of its workings. It is one of the points in favour of the genuineness of MacGregor Mathers' claims that he wrapped himself in the most impenetrable secrecy and could not be tempted out from his shell even in self-defence.

The evidence concerning the sources from which MacGregor Mathers obtained his MSS is, so far as I have been able to sift it, inconclusive and conflicting, and a good deal has been said about those MSS which cannot be substantiated. But that those MSS exist I can vouch for as a fact, because I know reliable people who have actually seen them; but as they were in cipher, my informants were not much the wiser, nor could they say how much MacGregor Mathers got out of them, and how much he added on as original work.

To get accurate information on the subject was not easy, especially as I came on the scene late in the day, after MacGregor Mathers' death, and it was rather like trying to obtain evidence concerning the nature of the cloth from which were made the robes of the King with No Clothes On. Everybody pledged their immortal souls as to the truth of the legends that were current in the Order that he founded; accepting them uncritically as they circulated by word of mouth and gained authority from much repetition.

So far as I could see, from what I could learn of the matter and what I saw of the people concerned, MacGregor Mathers had a wide range of rare but not very accurate or profound knowledge, in which professional scholars were able to pick holes; but in him were the roots of the matter, for he saw the mystical and philosophical significance behind what he had reaped in the queer fields of Alchemy, the Qabalah, and Egyptology. To him came, by the curious concatenation of invisible forces that are called chance, the famous cipher MSS, and in them he found the formulae which formed the basis of his rituals. These gave him the keys to the queer mass of crazy metaphysical ironmongery which he had already discovered to be a lock. He inserted the psychic key in the metaphysical lock, and lo! it turned and the door of the supernormal consciousness was flung open.

How much of the ceremonies were given verbatim in the cipher MSS, and how much was contrived by Mathers out of his knowledge with the aid of the keys with which the MSS supplied him, I do not know; but I am quite satisfied, from my experience of them, that the system he worked contained factors quite out of the ordinary, which were not the fruits of pure scholarship, however recondite. If MacGregor Mathers was the sole original author of that system, then he was one of the world's greatest men; but from what I saw of his Order, I do not think he was that.

The effect of the ceremonies and methods taught by MacGregor Mathers was to produce the most remarkable psychic experiences and extensions of consciousness in those who had any psychic capacity at all; the methods and aim of these processes were intelligently taught in the higher grades in certain sections of this Order, and it was possible for those so instructed to produce the results at will, and the effect of repeated experiments was cumulative. They obtained, in fact, by psychic methods, the same results other people achieved by the use of such drugs as hashish and mescal, and without the disastrous after-effects that result from 'loosening the girders of the mind' by physical means.

In the light of the experience thus gained, the ancient Mysteries became comprehensible, and the possibilities of psychic work thus unfolded were simply limitless. Individual students varied enormously in their capacity to employ the means placed at their disposal; some were merely futile; some were dry-as-dust scholars, frightened out of their lives of obtaining any practical results from the formulae, and some became genuine adepts with signs following. Among the latter was Aleister Crowley, who has written upon occultism under his own name and various pseudonyms, among other, the Master Therion, Frater P., Perdurabo, and a varied assortment.

Some ten years before I came in touch with Mathers' organization there were wars and rumours of wars. The truth of the matter is hard to come by, but when both sides claim to be angels opposed by devils, it is probably a case of six of one and half a dozen of the other. Anyway, as a result of the quarrel, Crowley published the bulk of MacGregor Mathers' secrets in his magazine, *The Equinox*, and Mathers cursed Crowley with bell, book and candle.

The Order suffered severely during the first World War, and Mathers himself died in Paris from influenza during the epidemic. When I came in touch with his organization, it was manned mainly by widows and grey-bearded ancients, and did not appear to be a very promising field of occult endeavour.

But I had had considerable experience of practical occultism before I made its acquaintance, and I immediately recognized power of a degree and kind I had never met before, and had not the slightest doubt but that I was on the trail of the genuine tradition, despite its inadequate exposition. For some reason best known to themselves, the elucidations and interpretations had been withdrawn into the innermost Inner by the secret chiefs, who simply sat upon them like broody hens on china eggs. The organization had broken up into a number of *disjecta membra*, and everybody regarded everybody else with suspicion as not being of the true orthodoxy.

I, for my part, took no part in the human pettinesses of the mundane plane, but worked at the system, and the system yielded fruits. Other people, I think, must have done the same, among them, Mr Regardie. At any rate, in his two books, *The Garden of Pomegranates* and *The Tree of Life*, he teaches the Golden Dawn system as I learnt it in the various branches of the Order of which I have been a member.

Mr Regardie acknowledges his indebtedness to MacGregor Mathers and Wynn Westcott, but he only quotes from their published works. He quotes so extensively from Crowley, especially from his four-volume work, *Magick*, in which is reprinted the best of the *Equinox* articles and some additional material, and his viewpoint so exactly expresses the best aspects of Crowley's teaching, that I conclude that Crowley's Order, the A.A., not Mather's G.D., is his source. The A.A., however, drew its magical system from the G.D., therefore for all practical purposes Regardie is using the Mathers' system, just as I am myself.

Regardie's two books I unhesitatingly recommend; *The Tree of Life* in particular is a magnificent piece of work, in my opinion the best book on magic that has ever been published. Crowley's *Magick*, of which Regardie makes much use and to which he acknowledges his indebtedness, is also very valuable to the student, but only the advanced student could use it with profit. It is very uneven in its literary quality; contains much grossness and ribaldry, like all Crowley's writings, and much of it is deliberately obscure and allusive. The formulae, too, on which he works, would be considered averse and evil by occultists accustomed to the Qabalistic tradition, for he uses 11 instead of 10 as the basis of his batteries of knocks in the magical ceremonies, and 11 is the number of the Qliphoth, or Evil Sephiroth; a battery of 11, therefore, is an invocation of the Qliphoth. No hint is given of this in the text, and it is an ugly trap for the unwary student.

Crowley also gives the North as the holy point towards which the operator turns to invoke, instead of the East, 'whence light arises', as is the classical practice. Now the north is called 'the place of greatest symbolic darkness', and is only the holy point of one sect, the Yezidees, or devil worshippers. It is obvious, therefore, that the student who is rash enough to experiment with a battery of 11 knocks and an invocation to the north, is not going to contact what most people would consider to be desirable forces.

Crowley has, however, a remarkable insight into the philosophy of occultism, and when he expounds this, he is a most illuminating writer, and I, for one, would not wish to minimize my debt to his writings;

his practical methods, however, are another matter, and are, in my opinion, too dangerous to meddle with in any shape or form.

If I read the signs aright, MacGregor Mathers, Crowley, Regardie and myself are all working on the same formula, the formula contained in the mysterious cipher MSS discovered by Mathers; Regardie draws from Mathers via Crowley; I imagine, however, that he is alive to the alterations in the formulae that Crowley introduced, for they do not appear in his books, and the formulae he gives are the ones familiar to me in the Golden Dawn workings. These I have found to be sound and effectual; Crowley's version of them I consider to be averse and destructive, though I cannot speak from personal experience on the subject, as I have never had any dealings with his method. I have talked with a number of people who have, however, and there seem to be no two opinions on this point after a sufficient time has elapsed to allow end-results to be seen.

But while I entirely dissociate myself from Crowley's methods, I would not wish to minimize his contribution to occult literature, which is of the highest value. From his books the advanced student, who knows how to read between the lines and refine the gold from the dross, can learn an immense amount, and if our interest is limited to an author's writings, we need not concern ourselves with his personal character or private life.

One of the most difficult problems in occultism today concerns the question of authority. What constitutes a genuine initiation? In what does a genuine occult Order consist? Who and where are the Masters? We need to answer all these questions unequivocally and to define standards of judgment before we can put one foot before another on the Path. I do not propose in these pages to discuss these questions in detail, for I have done so elsewhere, but I shall make a definite attempt to define a standard of judgment in occult matters that shall enable an opinion to be formed in specific cases.

Authority which is wrapped in mystery is a thing that is singularly liable to abuse, and it is very difficult to see how, in the absence of persecution, it can have any justification. When occultism had to be pursued at the risk of life and liberty it was a different matter, but why in the name of common sense should any occult organization burrow underground at the present day? Individuals may find it wise to conceal their interest for professional or social reasons, but it is difficult to see why any professed occult teacher should make a secret of his doings save for the reason that human nature loves a mystery and a modicum of theatricality enhances his prestige. But the dedicated initiator, and none other is worthy of consideration, looks upon esoteric science as a philosophy and a religion, and has no use for such banalities, leaving them to the quack, who finds in mystery-mongering an effectual form of publicity.

We may take a sponge, then, and wipe clean off the slate any individual or organization which cannot or will not put the cards on the table and reveal its antecedents.

It is an unfortunate thing that popular taste has been fed on occult marvels to such an extent that the wholesome fare of actual fact has become repugnant to it. Unless the spiritual ancestry of an order or an initiator is remote both in time and space, there is no prestige. The charlatan takes advantage of this, and reaps the harvest of claims which it is as impossible for us to examine as it is for him to substantiate. Whatever it may be in the East, the lines of contact on the physical plane in the West have been so utterly broken and destroyed with historical time that they have to be pieced together like ancient pottery. Experience proves, however, that when a certain amount of piecing has been done and the pattern appears, it is possible for the psychic to pick up the inner plane contacts and reforge the link. This is what is actually done in the modern Mysteries.

Because an initiator or an organization claims descent from the Himalayan Brotherhood or the Rosicrucians, or any other of the much-advertised secret Orders, it does not follow that that descent is by an unbroken line of tradition on the physical plane; neither does it follow, even if there is no such line of descent, that the claim is invalid. It is possible for an occultist of a certain degree of development to pick up the psychic contacts of these great inner plane organizations and to be working under their influence. When this occurs, very curious things happen on the physical plane, and the worker finds that he is constantly picking up the broken fragments of the tradition to which he is dedicated.

In my own experience I can see, on looking back, that for at least three years before I came in touch with it on the physical plane, I was working on the contacts of the Order into which I was finally received. These contacts I also picked up at different points on the two occasions when they had been totally severed on the physical plane. One appears to be running on invisible rails when once the contacts of one of the great Fraternities had been picked up. There is a large body of testimony to bear witness to this fact.

An occult Order might be likened to an iceberg, of which one-seventh floats above the surface of the water and the rest is submerged. Six-sevenths of occult work is performed on the inner-planes, and of that, five-sixths consist of subjective experiences. The vital thing, then, for any student or initiator, is to have the inner plane contacts of a valid Order; given these, the outer aspect will begin to crystallize around it in the same way as the pearl is laid down layer by layer round the grain of sand in the oyster's shell.

But although the inner plane contact is the vital nucleus, any student or initiator would be in a poor way if he had no body of mundane knowledge to draw upon. The occult systems are too intricate and too detailed for their psychic discernment to be a practical matter.

A great body of tradition exists, though scattered and concealed, and the student in whom the inner eye is open can penetrate its significance when he studies it. If he aims at being an initiator and training students, it is necessary that he should codify this knowledge and reduce it to an intelligible system; the value of an occult school depends in large measure on the manner in which this purely mundane work has been done. The Ancient Wisdom must be correlated with modern thought if its significance is to be made available for the student.

An occult school, then, needs to contain psychics who have the living contacts and scholars who have the relevant knowledge. Given these two things, ancient charters are of little significance; for unless the living contacts are there, and unless the system has been kept up to date generation by generation, charters may be nothing but gravestones marking the burial-place of a dead faith.

Mystical organizations are not long-lived things; they seldom survive the generation that had personal contact with the founder. As soon as the original impulse loses its momentum, senility sets in, and they have to be reborn amid throes unspeakable. Old bottles will seldom hold new wine, and reform usually takes place by schism rather than by expansion and restatement.

If we seek the roots of living spiritual experience, we are unwise to look for it along the lines of organized physical plane tradition. The wind bloweth where it listeth, not where it is chartered by established authority. The real line of contact is a personal one, and works in a very peculiar, but very definite way. The connecting thread is of the slenderest, yet nevertheless it is there. It is like the grain of leaven that was worked into seven measures of meal—minute, indispensable and effectual. This indispensable physical plane link appears to consist in a personal meeting between the seeker and someone who possesses the inner plane contacts. In every record of the foundation of an Order we read of a meeting between its founder and an illuminated teacher who gave him his contacts by virtue of his personal magnetism.

Abraham, the father of the spiritual Israel, met that mysterious figure, Melchizedek, who came to him bearing bread and wine for the first Eucharist. Jesus, on the eve of His ministry, sought out John the Baptist, the last of the prophets of Israel. Christian Rosencreutz travelled to Damcar, or Damascus, in search of an initiator. Abramelin found the promised instructor among the hermits of the Egyptian desert. Rudolph Steiner met his teacher in the Black Forest. Mme Blavatsky met a certain Indian Adept in Kensington Gardens during the Jubilee celebrations. MacGregor Mathers found the mysterious cipher manuscripts and communicated with an address contained therein.

But let it be clearly noted that the personal contact with an initiated adept, though the turning-point of each career, was no more than a clue that had to be unravelled. Mme Blavatsky had to write her books and build up her organization. MacGregor Mathers used his unique scholarship to give visible body and form to the system of which he received no more than the keys. In each case the greatness of the work accomplished depended upon the calibre of the worker. There must have been many who contacted the teachers of these great pioneers and no doubt received enlightment according to their capacity, but who built nothing in the way of an organization and have left no mark on the world.

Be it noted also that each of the systems thus founded had wrought into their structure the inherent weaknesses of their founders, and these weaknesses formed the lines of fissure along which they ultimately crumbled. Mme Blavatsky had very little discerment where human character was concerned, and though her devotion to her ideals was unquestioned, she was singularly unwise in her policy and unscrupulous in her methods. The 'Back to Blavatsky' movement, in its condemnation of modern Theosophy, would do well to remember that the weeds to which they are putting the sickle are but the full growth of the seed she sowed in her unwisdom and lack of principle. MacGregor Mathers too, who had no other source of income than his esoteric school, steadily weakened it and finally broke it up by his suspiciousness and exclusiveness.

From these observed facts we learn several things that are of importance to us in forming our standard of judgment. We learn, firstly, that physical tradition, save in so far as it consists of the written word which can be studied, is not of supreme importance, because the real value of a long line of spiritual lineage is in the group mind on the inner planes, and this can be picked up by psychic contact even by those who are not the heirs of the mundane line of inheritance. Moreover, the legal heirs may most lamentably fail to keep the channels open, and so be blind leaders of the blind. Function, not charter, alone gives the right to work the Mysteries.

Secondly we learn that it is not enough to cry Lord, Lord, loudly and persistently; there must be an adequate equipment of scholarship and organization on the physical plane to enable the spiritual forces to find a channel. It has been truly said that the power of endurance of a faith depends entirely upon its literature. All the great faiths have as their nucleus a book, a Bible, a Koran, or the Upanishads. Whatever spiritual teacher relies upon oral teaching leaves no permanent record behind him. There must be a book, and a mystical or holy book, which speaks, not to reason and intelligence, but to intuition and faith. The specific statements of the Neo-Theosophical literature of the Besant-Leadbeater school, which attempt to enlighten and convince the conscious mind, are not the centre round which the movement founded by Mme Blavatsky is rallying its shattered forces; it is *The Secret Doctrine* which is the sacred book that will hold the movement together long after *The Lives of Alcyone* have been mercifully forgotten.

There must be a book, written under the influence of a powerful spiritual inspiration, which forms the permanent nucleus of any movement that is to survive its founder. Such a book exalts the consciousness of those who read it and puts them in psychic touch with the sources whence the inspiration came; they are then able to work independently. People are never satisfied to be spoon-fed indefinitely, and unless a system is able to give them these living contacts, it will fail to hold any but the young souls, and of such a movement cannot be built.

It will be interesting to see whether the mass of Rudolph Steiner's writings will afford such a book for his students. I am inclined to doubt whether they are quite of that calibre. MacGregor Mathers left behind him the superb rituals of his *Golden Dawn*, and these, with their mass of symbolism and magical effectualness, form an inexhaustible mine of inspiration to the initiates of his tradition, which in consequence rekindles its fires whenever there are eyes to see.

We have an inspirational nucleus in the *Cosmic Doctrine*. We also connect up with the Golden Dawn contacts. It has been our endeavour from the first to make our system self-acting and independent of personal teaching. At the present moment it is somewhat like an arterial road in course of construction—there are long stretches of broad highway, and there are bottle-necks and narrow bridges where construction work is going on. We believe, however, that we have the necessary nucleus of permanency in our system, and that it will survive the generation that saw its beginning, and permit of the expansion necessary to adapt it to the needs of future generations, because it depends on method rather than on doctrine.

Subversive Elements in the Occult Movement

The occult movement has always been an object of suspicion to the powers that be, and not unreasonably so, for the secrecy in which it tries to shroud itself naturally attracts more attention than it avoids; moreover, this very system of secrecy can conveniently be used as a cloak for other things than occultism, and has so been used on many occasions in the past. The occultist, therefore, cannot reasonably resent the suspicion he has aroused, but should endeavour, by all the means available to him, to clarify the situation, give proof of his *bona fides*, and so conduct his affairs that they shall not afford a cover to evil-doers.

The influences at work in the world today range themselves under two banners, as they have always done. The choice of a banner is a matter of temperament; it has been truly said that everyone is a Radical in his youth and a Die-hard in his old age. We shall always find that the timid, and those whom the god of this world has blessed, are on the side of conservatism, or the maintenance of the present state of affairs. We shall also find that the bolder spirits, and those upon whom the prevailing social system presses hardly, desire to bring about changes in the order of things, and sometimes radical changes. In both camps we shall find moderate men and extremists; this is also a matter of temperament.

These two contrasting types of temperament have difficulty in understanding each other's viewpoint, and the more extreme examples usually lack the imagination to be able to conceive that there can be a reasonable viewpoint other than their own; consequently relations tend to become acrimonious, and each party endows the other with vices it does not possess, or is run by only a small and unrepresentative minority. Self-interest also exacerbates the situation, for any gains on the part of one party can only be at the expense of losses to the other. The two camps tend to become armed camps, with a perpetual guerrilla warfare going on between them that occasionally develops into a campaign on a vast scale.

Within limits, both aspects are essential to the well-being of the body politic; so clearly has experience proved this, that a well-organized Opposition is considered essential to the transaction of national business.

But although the normal polarity of viewpoint is a wholesome check
on extremes of any kind, and a normal and inevitable development in
this universe which manifests through pairs of opposites, there are to
be found in both camps extreme viewpoints which pass all bounds
of equilibrium, and, to use again the language of the Qabalists, are
Qliphothic, because they tend towards Chaos. The Die-hard would retain
vested interests in his dead hand, regardless of changing conditions or
the welfare of the world as a whole; and the anarchist, in his disgust
with existing conditions, would destroy them from the foundations
upward, thus bringing down the house of life on his own head and leaving
himself without shelter while the rebuilding is in progress. Reasonable
men of both parties regard their own extremists with distrust and are
able to give both sympathy and respect to their opponents.

As we have already noted, the choice of a party is usually dictated
by temperament rather than intellectual conviction. Those who are to
be found in the party of change are usually of a more imaginative and
impressionable temperament than those who find their spiritual home
in conservatism, using the word in its dictionary and not its political
sense. It is the same type of person who has an open ear for all things
new in any department of the world's activities; he is generally
unconventional in dress and diet; wears his hair long when other people
wear it short, as in modern times; and short when other people were
wearing it long, as among the Roundheads; and reacts violently to his
own complexes in general, not only in the things of his especial conviction,
but in all his way of life, whether in petty social usages or in the deeper
and more fundamental things of the spirit.

Occultism being, more than most things, an unconventional viewpoint, we find among its adherents a high percentage of the liberal-minded,
and comparatively few of those with a conservative or conventional
outlook. We must not, however, commit the logical fallacy of confusing
post hoc with *propter hoc*. People do not become radical in their views
because of any doctrines taught them under the veil of secrecy in occult
lodges, but become occultists because they are of the open-minded and
adventurous type.

There is, moreover, a certain type of the more philosophic reformer
who, in seeking an explanation which shall direct him to the root-causes
of social discontent, finds that the esoteric teachings afford that
explanation, especially in their doctrines concerning group minds, subtle
influences and evolutionary cycles. Such a social reformer studies
occultism, not for the purpose of applying ritual magic to his enemies,

as popular imagination supposes, but in order to understand root-causes.

It is rare to find the fanatic of either party in occult circles, or, for the matter of that, in any circles that do not see eye to eye with him; he has such a one-way mind, and is so concentrated on his special prepossession, that he is not interested in anything else, and has no time to waste on it.

It will be seen, then, that although people with advanced and unconventional viewpoints unquestionably predominate in occult circles, they do so incidentally and temperamentally, and not because the occult doctrines are immediately concerned with politics.

Occultism and the Underworld

Apart from what might be termed the genuine and sincere association with occultism with subversive persons and ideas which is purely accidental, depending upon the fact that the same type of temperament takes to both lines of interest, it cannot be denied that, inextricably mixed in with the occult movement is a dangerous underground line of subversive activity, and the authorities do well to keep a watch upon it. The peculiar, and quite needless, secrecy observed by occultists makes the occult movement a very handy cloak for various activities that will not bear inspection.

Scotland Yard is quite alive to this fact, and keeps a sharp eye on all occult organizations in consequence. The semi-public, semi-private nature of their proceedings fits them singularly well to the purposes of persons whose activities are under surveillance in their customary haunts. Any esoteric organization which is asked to allow letters to be sent in its care, or to receive parcels from printers to be called for by private car, or even to allow its telephone to be used by strangers, ought to be on its guard. It is an open secret that the letters of suspects are examined, and that their telephone calls are listened to; consequently it is of great importance to such persons to find unsuspected places where they can receive communications. There can very seldom be a good reason for not having letters sent to an accommodation address, and esoteric organizations which are complacent in this matter make difficulties for the whole movement.

It is a very unfortunate thing that the Theosophical Society became so intimately associated with Indian political activities, though in justice it must be said that there was probably no realization of what extremes these activities would ultimately lead to. Many people in consequence look upon all occult movements as being tarred with the same brush, and fear that they will be involved in all manner of complications if they become assoicated with them, and therefore limit their studies to the theory of esoteric science and find no opportunity for experience of its practice.

The Fascistically-inclined organizations of Great Britain seem to take the menace of subversive occultism very seriously, and to consider that an occult society is, *ipso facto*, subversive, and as such to be spied upon. No reasonable person should object to being inspected by the authorized representatives of law and order, because his own interests are protected in the so doing; but the amateur detective is an offensive nuisance, and as such, must expect just as short shrift as the Bolshevik.

The part played by drug addiction in the seamy side of occultism has been greatly over-rated. The drugs used are of the vision-producing type, such as anhalonium and hashish, and these are not drugs of addiction in the West. In the quantities in which they are used for occult experiments they are unlikely to do permanent harm.

The drugs to which people become addicts are those which either produce exhilaration and immunity to fatigue, or those which deaden consciousness and make a troubled life more bearable; under neither of these headings are to be found any of the vision-producing drugs. No one is likely to induce vision by their use sufficiently frequently to run any risk of addiction; and in any case, anhalonium is not habit-forming.

The risk to which these drugs expose those who use them is psychic, not physical; they may, if the experimenter is not an expert occultist, thoroughly competent in sealings and banishings, lay their user open to psychic invasion, and even obsession, because they open the doors of the astral to the unprepared consciousness, and as every swimmer knows, it is one thing to swim out, and another to swim back. I am not prepared to deny that they have a place in occult research, but such research should only be undertaken by those who are properly equipped, both as to their occult and their scientific attainments, and is in every way undesirable when done by those who are merely seeking a new thrill.

A great deal has been made by fiction writers of the Black Mass, which consists of desecrating by every means that an overwrought imagination can suggest, the sacred symbols of the Catholic faith. It is a procedure limited for all practical purposes to Roman Catholics, because, as Eliphas Levi pointed out, no one can partake of a Black Mass effectually who does not fervently believe in a White Mass. To the Nonconformist, the operations of a Black Mass would be senseless.

Sexual orgies have played a part in the Mysteries, and in the case of primitive peoples, we must not be too ready to condemn indiscriminately without considering the type of society in which they take place. Civilized standards cannot be used to judge primitive folk living under entirely different conditions and codes to ourselves. These orgies by no means necessarily produce the degeneration that missionaries would have us believe. They are by no manner of means the same thing as general sexual promiscuity, but are strictly limited to certain periods. A people living under natural conditions, in the most intimate touch with nature, and competing with plant and animal for the possession of the soil, has other social needs, and consequently other moral standards, than a highly organized, dense population, whose problem is to feed itself from a limited area. To the former, the orgies that stimulate fecundity may be as necessary and virtuous as the moral restraints of other types of society.

Nor must we make the mistake of thinking that because a race has either explicit or symbolic representations of the organs of reproduction among its sacred symbols it is necessarily licentious, any more than the fact that a nun is admitted to a religious Order with a marriage ceremony should lead us to suspect the same thing. Reticence in sexual questions is a matter of manners, not of morals.

There are truths in these things that we cannot ignore, and civilization is the poorer, and by no means either the cleaner or the healthier, for ignoring them. The trouble comes, however, when people who are licentiously inclined use them as a justification and a cloak. A certain amount of this has been done, especially on the Continent, in the name of occultism. For the most part, however, the loose-living in occult circles consists in a somewhat freely circulating assortment of 'soul-mates', and has no more occult significance than similar conditions in artistic circles. No magical use is made of the relationships; the only occult touch they have lies in the finding of justification for them in past lives, which no one except the persons concerned takes very seriously.

Various occultists, at different times, have attempted to put into practice the Freudian doctrines. No one with any insight into life can deny that there is a very large measure of truth in these doctrines, and that theoretically much justification can be found for the doings of such initiators. The social consequences, and the general strain and upheaval of such methods are, however, so serious that, whatever one may think of them from the point of view of pure science, in actual practice they are better left alone. For one thing, the forces employed get out of hand extremely easily, and when such practices are done in group formation, the group-mind takes on an atmosphere much too elemental to be tolerated by civilized people. Orgies and crude sexual magic have passed away from the level of consciousness at which civilized races function, just as infanticide and the despatch of the aged have passed away.

There are other, and better, methods of approaching the elemental levels of consciousness than these which do not belong to the Right Hand Path. By purely psychological methods the psychoanalyst achieves the same result; but it is only when the experience of the psychoanalyst is united to the knowledge of the esotericist that the deeper issues and supremest heights are reached.

At one time there was a widespread use of abnormal vice for magical purposes; the facts are well known and gave rise to repeated scandals. There is nothing to be said in mitigation of such practices; they are unnatural and destructive on every plane. There is reason to believe, however, that this phase of Black Occultism has had its day and is dying out. The principal exponent became hopelessly insane, and his example appears to have taught wisdom to such of his followers as had not learnt it from experience. Nevertheless, there remains a great deal of very unsound teaching and practice in certain circles, which produces a rich crop of psycho-pathologies. Group-minds have become tainted, and sensitive individuals are liable to very unpleasant experiences, to much psychic disturbance, and even to actual illness through association with them. The leaders of these groups are by no means given over to evil, but they have very little understanding of the forces with which they have been contacted. The repeated outbreaks of psychic trouble in their midst they attribute to occult attack from outside, or to the retaliation of the forces of evil against which they are contending, and do not realize that they are like people who have built their houses on the slopes of a volcano. However, it is probable that, with the breakdown of the leader, the atmosphere will gradually clear, and that which is of value will be disencumbered of the many unfortunate elements that have gathered about it.

The 'Jewish Peril'
There has always been a strong anti-Semite feeling among the continental nations, though in these islands it is of a very modified type. There have been books published recently which have set out to show that the revolution in Russia is the work of the Jews, and that the Jewish race, as an organized unit, is out to destroy civilization. Among these books are some which attempt to prove specifically that the Jewish initiate is a particularly dangerous person, and that any occult movement in which a goodly proportion of Jews finds a place must be a particularly dangerous movement.

In order to examine the rights and wrongs of this proposition we must first examine the basis on which it rests. What is the cause of the general antagonism to the Jew? Most people would say it was because they slew Our Lord, but the real answer to this question is probably to be found in the fact that there is a higher percentage of intellectual acuteness and ability, and a lower percentage of the martial virtues among the Jewish people than among most other races. This together with his racial pride and exclusiveness, irritates the Gentile; and as the Jew is seldom a war-like person, the irritation can safely be given free vent. Moreover, owing to his peculiar gift for finance, the Jew is the universal money-lender; and a very convenient way of putting paid to inconvenient debts is to have an occasional pogrom. Both parties possess strengths and weaknesses which makes them feared by, and yet a prey to, each other; such a state of affairs cannot be productive of mutual trust and good feeling.

It is perfectly true that in Bolshevism, and for the matter of that, in anarchical circles in general, there is a high percentage of Jews. The reason for this is not far to seek. The Jew is an exception to the general rule that an idealist is never practical. When an idealistic movement wants an efficient organizer, it generally fails to find it among the Gentiles in its ranks. The Jews have been the backbone of the Bolshevist movement for the simple reason that the Russian, left to himself, cannot organize and is hopelessly impractical, therefore the Jewish element has come to the front. This is not peculiar to the Bolshevist movement. Peter the Great, when reforming the Russian administration and founding the state upon modern lines, found it necessary to import German administrators for the simple reason that then, as now, the Russians could not organize or administer.

The Jew comes to the front in revolutionary circles, as he does in literary and scientific circles, owing to the high percentage of ability and driving-power to be found in his race. Again, *post hoc* is not *propter hoc*.

The Jew is attracted to the Western Esoteric Tradition because it is based on the Qabalah, the mystical wisdom of Israel, and because his intellect is of a type which takes kindly to esoteric philosophy. There appears to be a complete lack of the mystical element in Judaism to-day, save in relation to Jewish nationalism. For women, indeed, this is especially marked, for they have no place in the Jewish religion save as the carriers out of the Levitical customs that apply to the home. This lack seems to be keenly felt by the more thoughtful Jew, who feels the need of the kind of mysticism that Christianity teaches but cannot accept the Christ. He, and especially she, find this mysticism in occultism without any exclusive religious bias, and are able to adapt it to that which they honour in the tradition of Israel. Consequently there are many Jews in Western occultism, and, as always, they come to the front because of their intellectual capacity and driving-force.

It cannot but be obvious to anyone who looks at the matter in the light of history and racial psychology, that the Jewish race, as a race, has more to lose than any other by social upheaval and disorder, for they are the money-lenders of the world, and the first thing any nation does after a revolution is to wipe out back debts, both private and national. The Jewish race are, moreover, non-military; not that there are not individual fighting-men among the Jews, as the history of pugilism shows, but their peculiar religious tenets as applied to social customs make an army very difficult, if not impossible, to organize. Upon one occasion Jerusalem was stormed because the Jews would not work at its defences on the Sabbath.

There is no question, however, but that men of Jewish race have played an important part in determining the course of history by giving or withholding the sinews of war from bellicose monarchs and governments. This, however, has not been a matter of organized national policy, but of personal speculation and venture, at any rate since governments have ceased to force the Jew to lend money upon the security of his own back teeth. It is noteworthy that the record of the Jewish statesman is singularly clean; he serves the nation of his adoption with a single-minded integrity and conspicuous ability.

The Jew has always been prominent in Western occultism; in fact he was for centuries its only guardian, for the Church put down all speculation and experiment in spiritual things with a firm hand. The Qabalah has been the chief outlet for the spiritually-minded Jew who found phylacteries barren things; and the Qabalah has ceremonial magic and a highly technical psychism as its practical applications. In Israel is to be found the fountainhead of the Western Tradition; in fact Western occultists need to have a working knowledge of the elements of the Hebrew language in order to disentangle the barbarous jargon of dog-Hebrew which is the heritage of unscholary lodges.

The fanatic, who has got it firmly fixed in his head that the Jewish race is bent upon the destruction of all social order, looks upon it as one of the clearest proofs of the guilt of occultism that a Jewish element and influence is to be found therein. May we remind them, however, that the same may be said of Christianity, which has its cultural roots in Judaism. From the historical point of view, Abraham rather than Peter holds the keys of heaven for the Western world.

Esoteric tradition admits of no exclusiveness; it is the very essence of its spirit that it blasphemes no God that has been hallowed by man's devotion. It sees all religions as the expressions of man's spirit rather than the personal revelation of a jealous God to His chosen people. It suffers from neither superstitious awe nor bigoted fear. When asked to take sides in any acrimonious dispute concerning ultimate rights and wrongs it says, A plague on both your houses! The way of God is the way of the Lightning flash, zigzagging between the Pillars, and the place of equilibrium is in the central point of the Central Pillar.

11.

Esoteric Glossary

Teaching on esoteric subjects contains so many vaguely defined terms that it is advisable that those studying in our group should know more precisely what we mean when we use certain of the key-words. Indeed, in some of our earlier papers the meaning is not always as clear as it might be, as some time elapsed (as usually happens) before the need for these definitions became evident. We do not legislate for other groups but the definitions we give are in line with the principles behind our teaching and have now been shown by experience to be sound; it does not follow, however, that esoteric *publications* in general use the terms in exactly these meanings and, in fact, the same word with slightly varying signficances may sometimes be found in the same publication, making it necessary for the serious reader to be wary lest he gain a false impression, if indeed, the authors knew exactly the impression they wished to give.

The words we have in mind are set out below and in some instances information on the subjects is added.

The Logos is used as meaning the Solar Logos, the God of our Solar System. The God of the Cosmos we describe as The First Manifest.

The Manus are primarily 'ethnological' leaders on the Inner Planes of the great Root-Races. They depicted in themselves some great Idea or Principle which was behind the esoteric mission of their Root-Race. There is more than one type of Manu. The Manu of a Race is also the prototype or the Ideal Man of a Race, and in this connection the syllable 'MAN' in certain languages can be of extreme antiquity and significance. The Manus are of the First Three Swarms—Lords of Flame, Form and Mind— but not all of these Lords are Manus; the Manus are indeed of Archangelic type with *a 'multiple Ego'*. This is the nearest approximation in words to these great Beings. Their 'personalized' forms, however, appeared in 'humanized guise'.

The Masters are the perfected beings of the human evolution who guide mankind and perform certain other work rather than 'enter into their rest'; they are of various types and grades: They do not become 'Lords of Humanity' (see Cosmic Doctrine) until they have passed beyond all that is now known as humanity—even as no grade is established until the next is entered upon.

The Divine Spark may be thought of as the 'outer' aspect of the Cosmic Atom stamped with the Logoidal Impress. Until a high grade is attained it may be considered for all practical purposes as being the Cosmic Atom— the immortal part of each one of us, rooted in the Great Unmanifest, of the same *essence* as the Logoi, but vastly junior in development, etc.

The Individuality or Higher Self[1] is the unit of an evolution, consisting of the bodies of the highest three planes (using a seven plane system) organized around the Divine Spark.

The Lower Self, Personality, or Projection[1] is the unit of an incarnation consisting of the 'bodies' of the four lower planes (in a seven plane system). Its experiences are absorbed in essence after physical death by the Higher Self but this alone does not determine the next Projection as the Higher Self has phases of development between incarnations—based largely on pre-incarnatory (or involutionary) experiences which also influence the next Projection.

The Soul is one of the words most frequently used with differing meanings. We use it as signifying the inner aspects of the Personality plus the outer aspects of the Higher Self. It is, in fact, the unit of evolution up to a certain point (beyond Chesed).[2] The Personality aspects of it are (or should be) absorbed in essence by the Higher Self at death and the soul itself conditioned thereby for its next incarnation. (This is capable of much wider exposition.) It can be considered as the vehicle of evolving man as far as the Abyss on the Tree of Life and its state at death and after has much to do with the next Personality projected by the Higher Self. Certain 'pathologies' of an esoteric nature affecting future incarnations are possible from wrong actions and attitudes of mind by it during incarnation and after death.

Root-Races can be used for the original Race from which spring the sub-Races. It often refers to the seven great divisions of the Atlantean Race, and these racial prototypes were further developed in the post-diluvian world into the main racial 'families' as known exoterically. As a term 'Root-Race' can also refer to the four *colour* divisions of mankind, and also to the five stages of human evolution on this globe—i.e. the

---

[1] The Society of the Inner Light now uses the terms Evolutionary Personality and Incarnationary Personality, respectively.

[2] On the Tree of Life of the Qabalah.

Hyperborean, the Lemurian, the Atlantean, etc. The colour divisions and stages of human evolution also had Manus for there are many types of Manu. The White Race contains not only the most evolved—the Aryan—but also the Semites who were intended to bring yet another Ideal to the White Race. Thus did the Manu Melchizedek prepare the way for Jesus the Christ and thus did the idea of a Messiah become grafted on to the Semitic Tradition. (In the background of all this is a connection with the Holy Grail.) Behind the secret history of Israel moves the Archetypal Priest of the Atlantean-Semitic Root-Race; and owing to certain Atlantean errors the Jewish section of this Race have brought this Archetype to the West without themselves being fitted to use it, save for small groups. This is the 'Curse of the Jews' and dates from long before the birth of Jesus, though had they accepted him much would have been mitigated. Their theocracy should have grown into a World-State, but they would not share with others.

The Manus of certain Root-Races are known traditionally and some are enumerated:

RAMA was the Manu of the Aryan Race.

MELCHIZEDEK was the Manu of the Chaldean and early Semitic Races in addition to his Atlantean connection.

NARADA was the Manu of the First Atlantean Race.

ASURAMAYA was a Manu of an earlier Lemurian Race which had mingled with the early Atlanteans, and he 'lived' in Atlantis in these earliest days. He was the 'teacher of the starry wisdom' to the ante-diluvian world as was Melchizedek to the post-diluvial, and was the first astronomer. In Atlantis he worked with and under Narada. Euclid—who is a Lord of one of the Wisdom aspects of the Western Tradition (see 'Esoteric Orders') was not only a great human teacher but also had on the Inner Planes an aspect manifesting a direct 'beam' from Asuramaya (somewhat analogous but less in degree and origin, to the manifesting of the Christ by the Lord Jesus), which was more than an 'overshadowing'. This subject is too complex for further reference here.

The Semites were meant to be 'Priests of the Most High', but only a small section in a later evolution achieved this in a minor way. The Aryans were Magi and Colonizers.

The Archetypes are original patterns or models of a Divine Idea. Such archetypal (or archetypical) patterns are manifested in various ways:

(1)   Through the Divine or superhuman Instructors of certain races or nations on whose lives are based the dramatized rituals and the initiations of the various Mysteries.

(2)   Through non-human forms belonging to pre-terrestrial and pre-human types of development such as

(a)   The Signs of the Zodiac (in their actual, not anthropomorphized, form)

(b)   macrocosmic symbols related to the microcosm and based upon the Essential Forces of the Universe such as geometric and phallic ideographs of primary importance. These have passed into the human mind and emerge in dream symbolism but they are older than the human mind.

The traditional names of great archetypal figures are often racial memories of (1) i.e. of the Instructors—and belong to the different phases of evolution passed through by their groups; they originated with some shadowy teacher who had in ancient times guided some particular group. They should not be confused with the archetypal force of a Manu who worked upon the collective main 'family' of the whole race of which the group was a part. For example, Rama was the great Leader of the Aryan Race but Orpheus, Osiris, Isis, Odin, Merlin, etc., were Instructors of certain Aryan groups and ancestral memories of them passed into some of the gods and heroes of those groups. For, though some of the gods are 'natural forces' others are memories of prehistoric teachers. *Racial Angels* are high beings of the Archangelic or Anglic Hierarchy appointed since the beginning of the world as guardians of certain groups; they might be described as 'personalized principles of Archetypal Fire' who worked first with the Manus and then, on the withdrawal of the latter, continued in contact with the world as guardians of these principles and of the forces surrounding their 'earthing' (or establishing in Malkuth). Such a being is referred to in the Biblical phrase 'the Prince of the Powers of Persia', a great Racial Angel of a former period. Racial Angels guide races to the territory where they shall take root and as long as a nation remains sufficiently strong (in many senses of that word) the Angel is as its Higher Self so to speak. When that nation decays to such an extent that real contact with the Angel is not possible the Angel withdraws to a nation more capable of expressing the inner Principle he represents. Such Angels will incorporate in their 'realm' lesser tribal beings of other nations which become deeply integrated—by conquest or otherwise—with the original territory. The subject is very complex but will repay study;

conquest on the physical plane does not always triumph over a nation.
Anima and Animus.   These psychological terms are well defined in text-
books and reference should be made to such books—such reference is
especially needed for psychological expressions, many of which are already
used widely and inaccurately. All that need be said here is that Jung should
be read with great attention since it is probable he knew more than he
cared to express plainly. *When* integration with the Higher Self draws near
it is possible that 'anima' or 'animus' may give place to ideal figures of the
same sex as the Personality and such figures may even be foreshadowed
at a much earlier stage in sensitive people in the *higher* emotional states.

The Shadow—The Dweller on the Threshold

The 'Shadow' of Jungian psychology should not be confused with the
'Dweller on the Threshold'. The Shadow represents the subconscious
material of the present incarnation, of one life only, though, naturally, ·
it is affected by previous lives. The 'Facing of the Shadow' implies the
realization of the reality of the subconscious mind and the acceptance
of material often at variance with that of the conscious mind. It occurs,
therefore, at a comparatively early stage in the integration process—
corresponding on the Tree of Life to the 32nd Path (the Well) and to Yesod.

The 'Dweller on the Threshold' as used in our terminology represents
the *entire* past of the individual, all that has gone to make him what
he is. It is, therefore, the aggregate of *all* his 'Shadows'. The 'Facing of
the Dweller on the Threshold' is the confrontation with the entire past
and calls for the full acceptance of that past and of all that has gone
to make the individual what he now is. It occurs at a late stage in the
integration process. On the Tree of Life it would correspond with a
Chesedic initiation whose realizations are completed in Daath where
'Past becomes Present'. The full implication of the 'Dweller on the
Threshold' is probably not explicitly set out in psychological writings.
It should be noted that the integration here referred to is not the minor
one (so to speak) of Tiphareth but a much more complete one which
is nowhere fully treated of in published material as far as we know.

The 'Dweller on the Threshold' may be seen in vision by those who
have such experiences and should not be mistaken for an angelic or
Elemental figure of the usual type. It is a manifestation of the *aggregate*
debt in a personalized form or may arise from an awareness of that debt,
the forms varying in accordance with the nature of the debt. This 'vision'
or 'awareness' must be encountered before the really deep integration
and more advanced spiritual progress can be made. It is possible that it

will absorb the unregenerate side of the Personality (the 'renegade' image or aspect), and something approaching this modern teaching was depicted by the Egyptians in their figure of 'The Eater of Hearts'. Terrible as can be the Dweller on the Threshold to confront, it is yet only an 'averse' aspect of the Higher Self ('potentially', or 'unabsorbed') and can have something Divine in its appearance for it is connected with the suffering of the Higher Self which 'becomes sin' to redeem its projections—a consideration which merits deep meditation. In short, the Dweller on the Threshold is the sum-effect of the individual's past lives, his own averse character rising out of him into seemingly independent life.

The Masters (further to previous reference)
Just as at certain periods the esoteric work and position of individuals in incarnation are assessed so is the work of the Hierarchy assessed in its relation to the Greater Whole. It should be clearly understood that a Master is one whose function relates to the Solar Logoidal evolution and the Masters should be realized for what they are and their type of functional power understood. In order to function fully in the Solar Logoidal evolution much Cosmic growth has to be made—the 'Stellar Initiations' in all their gradations must be completed.
Racial Symbols—Animal. The Race-Soul exudes an 'influence' based on an aspect of its character and this 'influence' can assume an etheric form; it is a kind of 'totem'. As the Race develops this becomes one of its especial symbols. The symbol of Britain in this respect—originally of both Celts and Saxons—is a White Horse. The Lion as a symbol is not so early in origin nor so important being of Norman and heraldic derivation. The White Horse is a very ancient symbol and, if considered as a development of the Eo-Hippos has contact with Atlantis. No special posture—such as 'rampant', etc.—is prescribed.

Archetypal Forms and Psychology (see also above)
It is possible, for convenience in use, to divide types of Archetypal Forms into: (1) The Macrocosmic Archetypes such as the Gods which are 'personalizations' of great macrocosmic forces, (2) The Microcosmic Archetypes dealt with in modern psychology which are personalizations of the macrocosm in the soul of man. The Microcosmic Archetypes—such as the Father, Mother, Magician, Wise Woman, etc.—represent the linking of the developing soul with certain 'lines of force' in the macrocosm, or, in other words, the bringing of the manhood to God or the gods. (In this way behind the Masters is the Supernal Force that

may be described as 'The Great Sacrifice' and which is linked with the
Sacrificed God of the Tree of Life.)

In addition to the Archetypes here mentioned there exist what might
be called 'complementary forms' of various aspects of the Microcosm,
such as the Angel, the Daemon, etc., and the distressing type of Magical
Body ensouled with Elemental essence variously called the 'Dweller on
the Threshold', and the 'Evil Genius'. It is possible for these to represent
whole groups or families but detailed discussion of them here would
be too long and difficult for a paper like this; the psychological term
of 'the Renegade Aspect' or the psyche is applicable to them.

The Contrasexual Image. This is a well-known psychological
phenomenon; when recognized for what it truly is it can be a special
link between the Personality and the Higher Self, being an aspect of the
Angel of the Pillar opposite to the physical sex—that is female for the
Silver Pillar, male for the Black Pillar. (These Pillars refer to the composite
glyph of the Tree of Life and the Pillars—a Qabalistic symbol.)

Notes on the Grail and Kindred Symbolism

Contacts and power from the Inner Planes are received on the physical
plane either through a group or through an individual who passes on
to a group his own contacts made on their behalf. The former method
was the basis of the Old Testament Grail—the Ark, the latter was the
basis of the New Testament Grail—the Cup or Chalice. Both these
receptacles have become symbols, as have other forms of such
receptacles—the Dish, the Bowl, the Stone. Before these became symbols
they were facts. The Ark actually held a substance of the Inner Planes
which made a direct contact between God and the Group. In Atlantis
the Cup or Bowl was the Moon-Bowl (of the *old* Moon and the earliest
stages of mankind) in which was a substance in actual contact with the
Supernal. These 'substances' are Mysteries and, indeed, a version of what
in far later days was known as 'the Real Presence', and from memories
of them have been developed the sacramental rites of various creeds.
The finding of the Cup which had been withdrawn from man because
of his sins is behind the Grail legend in which the Cup of the *actual contact*
with the Innermost rather than the Cup as a symbol of that contact
appeared to certain persons. There are endless possibilities in meditation
on this theme, but much can be pieced together from what has already
been said. We think of Melchizedek bringing back the sacramental symbol
to Abraham; that his home was on Venus-Lucifer and that there is an old
legend that the Grail was fashioned from an emerald fallen from Lucifer's

crown. The Cup, however, was the ancient Atlantean contact with God stored within the 'Moon-Bowl'—it did not hold 'wine' in the literal sense. The Lord Jesus (a 'high-priest after the Order of Melchizedek') re-instituted it (as at their own levels did such saviours as Orpheus, Mithra, etc.). Behind all this is the *secret* history of Israel in the background of which moves the Archetypal Priest of the Semitic Atlantean Root-Race.

Sundry Notes on Astrology

1. The Zodiac comes under the influence of the (12) Cosmic Rays, and the true Zodiacal influence upon the human being dates not from that operating at the moment of the birth-date of his present incarnation but from the Cosmic 'groupings' in action at the time when the Divine Spark coming down the planes (see 'Cosmic Doctrine') was impressed with some special Zodiacal force. This force, if truly discerned, would be apparent in the astrological positions of each incarnation—also it would be possible to make of the individual influences at work on the Spirit a calculation somewhat analogous to that of the Precession of the Equinoxes at work on the Sun; the subject is difficult and calls for expert and specialized knowledge. Each Divine Spark is respectively influenced by one of the twelve great 'Concepts of Truth' which are behind the twelve Great Rays. This is the real fundamental astrology which covers an evolution. The working of the Lesser Zodiac during one incarnation is trivial by comparison, though its understanding can be very helpful.

2. The Zodiac is not so much an imaginary belt as 'zones' or 'rays' of influence touching the Earth at certain seasons. It is best considered in sets of four constellations. The three modes of force—Cardinal, Fixed, Mutable—refer to the three Rays of Life; there are three sets of these balanced with the Three Rays of Destruction. Each Zodiacal mode is aligned with one of these Rays of Life. The Rays of Life and the Zodicacal Signs equated with them vary with each evolution: the Four Holy Creatures of the present evolution did not rank as such before this evolution—despite the influences they shed. In the next evolution the four 'Mutable' Signs will be 'holy'. The Signs of the Zodiac are the mystical basis of the Cosmos.

3. The sun's passage through the Zodiac resembles the 'gathering of the limbs of Osiris', that is to say the building into the Individuality of the experiences gained from the various incarnations. These may be considered in one way as 'types of evolution' on the Path. Arthur's knights, the Twelve Apostles, and similar groupings may be thought of as allegorical figures in this way as well as historical facts in some instances.

If we regard the Sun-power in the horoscope as having the four aspects of horizon, zenith, sunset, and nadir, and as acting through not only the solar Sign itself and that on the ascendant but also through whatever Sign or Planet is on the cusp of the 10th, 7th, and 4th Houses respectively, we find that this is reflected in the initiate's horoscope by the four great Egyptian aspects—Ra, Osiris, Tum, Khepra. The Sun itself is a reflection of Sirius; Venus eventually is transcended in Sothis (Sirius) the home of Isis.

4.   Evolutionary changes are already beginning in the Cosmic spheres. Towards the end of an Evolution (covering a vast expanse of time) form itself begins to alter—as happened at the end of the Atlantean Age. At such a time great Cosmic Beings take over from those previously in charge and the 'outer' conditions of earth and man begin to change, largely because of 'rays' or 'influences' from distant stellar forces coming into operation.

Higher/Lower Self Contacting and Martyrdom

The Higher Self contacts the Lower Self in many ways. At first, contacts are rare and for the 'once-born' may happen only once or twice in a lifetime, showing as an intuitive awareness before some important event. A martyr is always an initiate in some degree even without any esoteric experience or training: in such a type a very deep conviction may be sent down by the Higher Self which must be acted on at all costs by the Lower Self even if suffering and death result. The Higher Self is not, of course, concerned with what the Lower Self understands as the rights of religion or politics but is occupied with some karmic matter to be adjusted by the Lower Self's death or by some motive arising out of Cosmic Law quite unknown to the Lower Self, veiled behind some doctrine or concept. The martyr may well seal with his blood a cause of which in the Lower Self he is quite unaware.

The Glyph of the Crucifixion (considered from two aspects)

1.   A most important symbol is that of The World-Soul and its Crucifixion. Our Lord 'concreted' or 'earthed' this glyph in his type of death. The World-Soul, however, is crucified on the Cross of the Elements, a cross which is continually expanding its arms through evolutionary development and, in material matters, through scientific research. The Elemental Cross has to reach its utmost limits of expansion in the present world and at the same time have each arm in perfect balance with the others. The *macrocosmic* Mother of Sorrows and the Great Teacher on either side of the World-Soul on the Elemental Cross make up this great

glyph. *Microcosmically* these are represented by Our Lady and St John on either side of the Cross of Calvary. Thus the 'dark aspect' of Binah (Ama) is a standing figure (the 'white aspect', Aima, is a seated figure). The hymn '*Stabat Mater Dolorosa*' is very significant for it is in form and force a Binah[1] rite, even to its three-fold rhyming structure.

Sorrow in the *macrocosm* implies realization of the Great Law, but in the *microcosm* it implies non-realization. Nevertheless, the deeper the capacity for feeling sorrow, the deeper is the realization eventually achieved.

2. The Universe is a Logoidal thought-form and its development is the unfolding, as it were, of a dream of God. Even as with man's dreams the Supernal Dream is 'interpreted' through a cypher of conditions analogous with what men call symbols. The cypher of this world is best described as a Figure on a Cross. The Logos is aware of Its creation in a a summarized form which gradually unfolds its meaning: Images such as this may be called 'Arch-Archetypes'. It does not greatly matter what name is given to the World-Symbol. It may be termed 'Spirit crucified on Matter', or 'Man on the Cross of the Elements', and may be aligned with the historic event near Jerusalem some 2,000 years ago. Such a Symbol is bound eventually to become esoterically connected with each one who achieves in this Evolution. The achievement is *first* made through a Redeemer who brings The Image to Malkuth; it is *finally* made by the individual in an individual sense. On each side of the World-Soul stands a figure—one is of the Virgin-Mother who brings forth in sorrow both to generation and regeneration, the other is the Mind of the World-Soul who watches beside it to give it courage and help and is the symbol of the Guides and Masters. Christian history has taken Our Lady and St John as the representatives of a vast Cosmic glyph which existed *before* Time. Nevertheless these representatives, being aligned with the glyph *in Time*, become themselves 'glyphs of the glyph'.

The coming of the Cosmic Christ in the Aquarian Age, the return of the redeemed 'Merlin', 'Arthur', and the Arthurian Figures in the Racial spheres refer to the time when man himself will take on the remains of his karma not dealt with by the last Great Redeemer. This individual karma—be it understood the least part of the karma—must be fully realized in order that it may be abreacted. Our Lord took on himself what may be described as the 'mass disbalance' of the whole Evolution and the aspects of individual sin which were clogging the Machinery of the Universe. The weight of *million of years* of sin was, therefore, laid on the Divine Scapegoat who

[1] See *Tree of Life*.

abreacted it in the short time we know of. This achievement shows the vast importance of realization compared with the relatively slight value of time itself. It is vitally important to understand what REALIZATION is and that it has little connection with physical plane timing. True realization in its myriad degrees of intensity implies some measure of definite abreaction of karma and the rending of the Veil between man and his Cosmic origin; this Veil was interposed in the Lemurian Age by the Lemurian Sin. Before this Sin and the differentiation of the sexes in evolution the human being consisted of the Higher Self in touch with the Divine Spark; there was no Personality as we now know it. The first 'projections' from the Higher Self as we now understand them were evolved around the 'Ego' created as a result of the Lemurian Shadow.

Notes on Madness, Lemurian Sin, etc.

The Aquarian attitude towards madness will be very different from the Piscean which has been accompanied by so much shame and embarrassment. It has been considered a terrible thing to have a member of the family in an asylum, but in the Aquarian Age far more people will be treated openly in mental hospitals and many will go there of their own free-will. Healing in the Aquarian Age will be more directed to mental conflicts and troubles rather than physical disease. This is connected with the beginning of the final dissolution of the separateness of the 'Ego' and with the right understanding of the Ring-Chaos.[1] Madness implies a refusal to accept the reality of the Ring-Chaos as a thrust-block, and the denial of the need to accept and seek Change. It is a very severe visitation of the forces of the Holy Third Sephirah (Binah) for the forces of the Dark Mother (Ama) and of the Ring-Chaos are one. The dissolution of the Ego is the Third Birth and involves an esoteric, deliberate and fully-controlled 'going out of one's mind' into the Cosmic Whole. Any refusal to accept the dissolution of the Ego will entail mental disorder for, at that stage, if the Ego is not obedient to evolutionary Law it could become so inflated that it would burst its boundaries involuntarily and out of all conscious control. It might be said that the difference between madness and the Third Birth is that in madness the Ego bursts its boundaries involuntarily, and in the Third Birth the Ego with knowledge and dedication is consciously dissolved—there is a conscious deliberate 'rending of the Veil' and the adept takes up his work as an evolved part of the Greater Whole, 'individual' but not 'separate'.

The 'Lemurian Shadow' was fundamentally the 'Sin of Separateness'.

[1] See *The Cosmic Doctrine*.

In the beginning it was intended that evolution should proceed by the experience of differentiation as a result of the epigenetic factors in the Atoms (using the terminology of the 'Cosmic Doctrine'), but the result of the Lemurian Sin was the separation of the Higher Self from the lower vehicles and physical form, having, as one of the many bad results, the loss of memory of the higher states of consciousness. The Divine Spark (or Logoidal Consciousness) could not prevent this as it cannot upon its own plane provide the formative aspect needed for manifestation. The physical plane manifestation, therefore, developed 'Ego' consciousness—the consciousness of a *separate* being. If there had been 'differentiation' and not 'separation' the resulting consciousness would have been that of 'individualization': much lies in the understanding and realization of the difference between what would have been the 'individualization-consciousness' and what is the 'ego-consciousness', or 'separation-consciousness'. Man must eventually achieve 'individualization-consciousness' in which the Divine Spark, Higher Self and Lower Self will all be in harmonious function and the consciousness of the body of Malkuth be recognized for what it really is, a cell in the body of the 'Earth Mother'. A basic problem of the human evolution as the result of the 'Fall' is the conflict in the individual between the Elemental and Spiritual aspects of the One Life. In its severest forms this conflict leads to a kind of schizophrenia in which the Elemental life of the person becomes quite a separate existence from the spiritual.

Note. This subject is a very deep and difficult one. The language used and the ideas conveyed are as it were 'approximations'; that is to say they are intended to lead to an understanding of the subject rather than to give hard and fast definitions. These remarks apply also to the *Glyph of the Crucifixion.* Generally speaking such teachings of the Tradition are given to help the mind on to its own conclusions and realizations.

Pan as a Symbol. The 'Great God Pan' in the final understanding of him, is a Chokmah figure in the Solar-Logoidal System. He is a symbol that bears relation to the symbol of 'the-Serpent-that-holds-his-tail-in-his-mouth'. In the Great God Pan lies the understanding both of the beginning and ending of the sex-force. He represents the 'rousing of Kundalini' and he also represents that force used in the service of the higher magic of wisdom. Yet any figure that represents the beginning and the end conjoined is still a symbol and must eventually fade out to give place to Reality. The *Reality* of the Great God Pan can be nothing less than a part of the Solar Logos.

The saying 'all the gods are one god and all the goddesses are one goddess and there is one Initiator' should be constantly worked on. The 'one Initiator' is increasing realization as a result of the increasing integration of Higher Self and Personality which leads on to the 'Empty Room' in Daath. Therefore in varying degrees and upon different levels all gods and goddesses represent aspects of the One God which is both 'male' and 'female'.

Byron.   Non-human Forces sometimes overshadow humans and bring in influences of other Racial Groups than that of those humans. The various Racial Groups differ in their influences, hence the different types of Elementals 'seen' in various countries. Byron is an illustration of one influenced by Forces of more than one Racial Group. In addition he had a daemonic form of 'daimon' overshadowing his Higher Self and this daimon had no opportunity in that incarnation of manifesting save mainly through the intellect. The revolutionary forces at work in Byron's day were able to use this dynamic daimon to some extent but more than half remained unexpressed. Thus there is a sense of something 'tearing itself to pieces' all the time and having to do all it could with the utmost urgency since time was short. (The poet died at the age of 36.)

Form (In Binah and Yesod).   Binah represents the *concept* behind the Form and its Archangel represents the Intelligence behind Form, 'the Formless Builder of Form' working behind both the Dark and Bright Aspects. Yesod represents the etheric mesh of Form.

Healing and the Four Elements.   The Aquarian Age is specially concerned with 'Air-healing' through the use of the human mind and certain Forces of Air—hence Steiner's references to the value of the mistletoe, which is an Air symbol. In this Age in addition to the special Air aspect the healing values of all Four Elements should be re-established and the power of each be realized. In each Element there are harmful as well as healing Forces. The great healers of former Ages worked mainly through a certain 'ray' of the Sun and upon different levels of that ray. Our Lord used this solar ray by bringing it down through himself on to others. Other solar healers used another level of this ray and brought it into contact with the patient's Higher Self whence it approached his Personality; they were not, of course, able to contact it in the major degree of force used by Our Lord.

Archetypes (refer also to previous notes).   It must be remembered that Archetypes, though possessing a certain defined aspect of force, work in phases. Thus the three great Logoidal Aspects (Love, Wisdom, Power) work each in three phases. For example, the Wisdom Aspect works through Wisdom-wisdom, Wisdom-power, Wisdom-love. In the development of an initiate there may at times appear to be a retrogression to a type of manifestation which was thought to have been left behind, but what really happens is that during initiatory development each Path is retraced upon a higher arc. Thus an archetypal force may again take up the work of past years but upon a higher level. The lower curve of a new spiral of evolution corresponds with the ascending curve of the previous spiral.

The Watchman (or Watcher on the Tower) is an archetypal figure sometimes used from the Inner Planes to help the soul to realize its true destiny. It represents the eternal indestructible part of each one—linking the Higher Self with the Divine Spark. It recognizes only Reality and therefore its actions seek to destroy all that hinders realization of a soul's destiny. The temporal part of each one is ultimately destroyed because it is unrecognized by the Watchman. He is a figure of Eternity, immovable, unchanging, belonging to the Past, Present and Future, making them one. He is a Daath figure, related to the Abstract Mind and Causative Planes.

Horus is sometimes called the Lord of the Aquarian Age. He is a winged complete being containing within himself his father Osiris and his mother Isis. Isis and Osiris were one being in primeval days and later split into two. Their son represents each on the new arc—joined once more into one being. Thus Isis and Osiris represent the primal good Lemurian Age and Horus represents the completed Aquarian version of that Age raised to a spiritual level—hence the wings.

Earth-bound Souls. Earth-bound souls can, broadly, be divided into two types.

1. The type of soul who, by reason of karmic implications, has strong contact with Earth conditions.

In the phase following physical death, such a type can easily be drawn back because the 'earth' vibrations are stronger than the spiritual body of the soul until after the lapse of a certain amount of time in which the spiritual body can be built up for activity on the higher and more subtle planes. This is one of the reasons why 'angels' attend at a man's death—they protect him during the phase of adjustment to the new conditions, their vibrations help him to move into a 'new mansion'.

If the soul is drawn back it is usually due to weakness in the ethical nature, or to a swamping by the earth forces due to special evolutionary, karmic factors in which it is involved—often in relation to others who still remain on the physical plane. Such souls are always helped on the Inner Planes by more evolved human beings as well as by angels.

2. The strong type of soul who, to suit his own convenience, wills to remain as close as possible to earth conditions, refusing to undergo the subjective experiences which will build up the spiritual body.

This type of soul realizes that without 'a body' the forces will begin to disintegrate, to diffuse, and that this will mean destruction to his way of life. He therefore puts up a tremendous fight, causing what is known as 'haunting', and can, in order to maintain himself, use obsession of animals and creatures of lower development. It is necessary for the Adepti to deal with such cases for the 'will' of a man is involved. If a case were so severe that the 'will' had to be broken the result would be disintegration of the human soul; the Adepti work to change the 'will' if at all possible. The unpleasant, frightening and sometimes dangerous symptoms of haunting are due to the fact that by virtue of his higher grade this departed human being can, for a certain period of time—until the higher Cosmic forces have built up a wall of pressure to prevent this—manipulate and control the vibrations of the 'earth' or of a lower type of being.

An Inner Plane Adept is handicapped in his work on this type of condition by not having a physical form to work with or through, because the higher forces, which are being brought down to build up the wall of pressure that will effectively seal the soul off from the earth contacts, need to be 'earthed' through a physical form. Otherwise the wall, however strong, lacks roots and the earth-bound soul of great strength will overthrow it. Also, a haunting is fed by fear. For these reasons, the Adepti need in such work the strong Adept on the Physical Plane of compassionate understanding. The Adepti on the Inner Plane deal with the Cosmic forces and the Individuality of the man; the Physical Plane Adept's co-operation is needed on the lower levels of the Earth's forces and the Personality of the man involved. If properly understood, such work has a regenerative effect on all who are in any way involved.

The Earth and Venus.   The Earth was 'incarnated' in the sphere of Venus at a very early phase. Consequently there is a contact between Venus and Earth.

Netzach has the Rose and the Lamp—two great Rosicrucian symbols—as its own, also it has the girdle or zone. Netzach has far more significance than as the sphere of 'romance'. Here are found three symbols used by the Rosicrucians, and here is the sphere from which the great Manu brought the three gifts to man.

The zone or girdle holds an inner significance of the Earth's contact with Venus. (The legend of the girdle of Ishtar—the last possession that the goddess was called on to surrender in the Underworld during her search for Tammuz—must have had deep spiritual meaning.)

The Earth contacted deep spiritual awareness during her Venus phase and from Venus spiritual teaching came to Earth in her present phase, through the Manu Melchizedek. Among the three Netzach symbols in the Mystical Qabalah and those three gifts of the Manu there is an inner alignment of meaning though not of form; the Lamp is thus aligned with Asbestos, for only when a man can withstand spiritual Fire and Water may he hold that Lamp in his hand. This is the sphere that contains the Lamp which holds and shows forth the Flame. The Flame is drawn from Chokmah and fanned by Geburah but shown to the Earth by Netzach. Netzach is, in one tradition, the source of the Grail—the emerald which fell from Lucifer's crown as he came to Earth.

Astrology. (1). It is said that the first formative forces streamed upon the Earth from the eye of the Constellation of Taurus—associated with Aldebaran.

(2). In the earliest Lemurian days certain Adepti came to Earth from the planet Jupiter which contains a 'secret scheme' connected with the Earth.

Racial Forces. In this Age, all Racial forces are undergoing changes; Racial Angels themselves are being influenced from more remote spheres by other Cosmic Beings.

When a man reincarnates, the Race to which he is sent is by no means a matter of chance, for the different lessons necessary and the different Karmic details to be worked out cannot always be found in the Race to which there may be a natural gravitation from past lives. In this fact we may find an understanding of 'the traitor', the 'aggressive pacifist' and such figures who have had, probably in the 1st incarnation, links with a Race which at that time were legitimate, but now may be out of place. The unevolved man is often swayed to some extent by his former Racial Angel. The more evolved man realizes that his duty is to his present Racial Angel but his past life may enable him to handle 'enemy' force in wartime with special skill.

Races nowadays are less defined through blood: they tend to be in categories of language, blood being more and more mixed. The influences of the territory upon which a Race was first settled continue as a subconscious element however, or, to put it differently, people of the same language fall heir to the forces of the land in which the language matured. The blood-bond represents the Element of Fire, to which indeed Racial Angels also belong. The language-bond represents the Element of Air. There is much to be learnt of this in the study of the occultism of speech. As time proceeds, we shall tend to draw back to one Root-Race and Europe is now tending towards this (and Britain is included). The Russian Race tends to the East and to join up once more with the Mongolian powers via Siberia. Behind these Mongolian powers are remote forces for good working from Tibet very gradually upon Russia.

The symbolic formula of Race and Language is the Tower of Babel. This Tower was built out of time and therefore had to be destroyed. It should now be built up, for now we tend rightfully 'to reach to the skies' and to have 'one language'.

Vanity. Apart from its more easily recognizable manifestations, vanity can be the result of a form of hate and distaste for the Personality by an 'averse' aspect of a Higher Self. In such a case the Personality of early days will probably be found to have been spurned by that averse aspect and the instrument provided for incarnation refused or its experiences rejected. A kind of hate can be directed all the time by what seems to be the inner levels of the Personality against the Personality itself, resulting in a slow and insidious form of suicide. Flattery or even comfort offered by others are not acceptable to this type of vanity which can consider only its own perverted reflection. Thus the perverted opinions of the false image or aspect biases all matters concerning that Self. Self-love and self-hate are two sides of the same coin.

Racial Angels (See also above)

These angels are evolving somewhat like the Higher Selves of human beings and have to move on to other stages of development, which in their case means working behind a different Race. As with men, the Racial Angel's main force may focus out of true alignment with its source and then very often an evil power will use the Racial Angel's force, even as an evil Personality will utilize the force of its Higher Self in wrong ways.

The Racial Angels may be compared to some extent with the Guardian Angel connected with the individual. These latter are embodiments of the Logoidal Will, split off into an entity attached to each human unit when spiritual differentiation took place. The Racial Angels are entities holding one of the especial aspects of the Manu who first guided the main branch of the Race. (Thus the Aryan Leader Rama has left aspects of his power in the various Aryan Races.)

The Racial Angels—when properly evolved—earn a seat at the sidereal Round Table. Every now and again, some political measure is introduced which marks this concept. Again and again also it is found that the seat will not be taken until after a long time—even as a man cannot sit at the Round Table until he is king of himself. Angels of large and backward races are not at the same stage as Angels of the relatively developed nations. There is a lack of cohesion in such racial vehicles which are normally not welded properly with the Group-mind. In such conditions a strong and scheming party may interpolate a 'false' Angel and this 'false' Angel takes the place of the true Racial Guardian, which was not strongly linked up to the Group.

Where several Races are amalgamated into one, the several Racial Angels are in one aura, and this aura may be regarded as one vast Oversoul. In this way the various feline groups are included in the Oversoul or aura of the Arch-Lion, and the Earth and the present Moon are parts of one Oversoul or aura.

Uriel and Sandalphon.   Uriel is the Regent of the Element of Earth, Sandalphon of the Sphere of Earth (Malkuth), and they have an interlinked relationship, each being Regent of a densest aspect of force. *Sandalphon* rules over the structure of the life-forms within this planet—thus he rules over the evolution of consciousness and of form upon the earth and so is Ruler of the 'Souls of Fire', which is a symbolic name for the consciousness of the atoms. *Uriel* rules over the basic forces of the earth itself, particularly the seismic powers, and was connected with this planet before man inhabited it. He has guided earth's evolution before its form solidified when it was passing through its fiery and watery stages. He is said to have foretold the Atlantean cataclysms and to have been the teacher of Enoch. Uriel brought the great Deluge—or, at least, administered it to the earth as a server of greater Powers. Through his agency Fire, Water and Air are esoterically 'permitted' to work upon earth. At one time Uriel was a Regent on the Old Moon and some of his power relates, therefore, to the Inner Earth.

The Inner Earth Potencies relate to the Old Moon (the moon which preceded the present planet) and to pre-Atlantean days when the human consciousness was somewhat of the nature of the Atziluth of Yesod. The Inner Earth is connected with a certain type of physical healing because it contains the first manifestation of the Four Elements and the primary components of the human body.

Raphael and Michael are each, at times, ascribed to the Sun. *Raphael* represents the basic forces of the Sun as he 'stands within the Sun.' *Michael* represents the solar forces in their aspect of spiritual power. Thus he directs one aspect of the power behind 'The Solar Hero'—whether god or demi-god or human and, representing the Supernal Fire, is in charge of the guarding of the approaches to consciousness from the Infernal Fire. He is ruler over the holy Beni Elohim. An 'unholy' section of these Beni Elohim helped in the Black Magic of Atlantis.

Endurance.   The esoteric concept of Endurance as a virtue is not in any way a form of the 'slave mentality'; it is the force of the rocks which *cannot* be moved and full awareness of that force.

Saturn, and a note on Animals.   The 'Saturn-evolution' of humanity was the Golden Age for Saturn was the first 'sun' of our humanity—not the Sun-behind-the-sun, but simply the first sun. Matter was then withdrawn from that planet and used on other planes and Saturn became the 'planet of Death and Constriction'. (The higher arcs of the Dark Mother deal with the breaking-down and building up of the debris of universes, i.e. Chaos.)

That was Eden or the Golden Age and its symbolism holds much interest. Saturn was connected with both solar and lunar developments of very remote Ages. Its magical metal is lead; to transmute this base metal into gold is a well-known symbolical alchemical operation. The *depth* of this symbolism lies in the fact that the lead must be turned *back* into gold. There is a mention in the Cosmic Doctrine of the star Alpha Centauri, and the star 'γ' (Gamma) of that constellation was that first contacted by the Logoidal Mind when contemplating the beginning of human evolution in *form*. The higher animals are developments of Logoidal 'experiments' which might have been human had not their Over-souls failed in certain points. The four highest types, however, have much part in the *design* of man—the Four Holy Living Creatures. Nevertheless, it was in the Centaur's sphere that something of the true design was reached. Hence the Centaur is a constellation of great import and the astrological equivalent if strong in a horoscope may indicate a special aptitude for the understanding of humanity. It is easy to see, also, how the deeply debased use of knowledge of these matters was a kind of evil inspiration to the Lemurian sinners.

Archetypes (see also above). The coalescing with a Cosmic Archetype is a very significant act. It means that a spiritual concept received from the Logoidal Mind becomes an actuality in Malkuth because it is lived out. This concept is first given to humanity in the form of a myth—and a myth may be likened to a dream of the Logoidal Unconscious which then becomes translated to a projection of human consciousness. Work on an Archetype helps a soul, group, or nation to redeem and assimilate an aspect of itself which had previously either been rejected or projected. Therefore there are many kinds of Archetypes, some dealing with the Personality specifically, some with the Individuality as well as the universal and Logoidal Archetypes, which can be applied to groups and nations. It is all part of the process of integration.

Pendragon. Arthur's symbol of the Dragon refers to Lemuria when the constellation Draco held the Pole Star. It becomes also either the Winged Serpent of the Higher Wisdom or the Evil Serpent.

Death, Change, Reincarnation, etc. The system of 'change'—which later became 'death'—was, at first, stages of withdrawal from the earth-plane; corruption of the physical vehicle had not as yet become stereotyped. The physical vehicle itself was hardly physical in the sense in which we now use the word; it was a densifying etheric vehicle which could be cast off somewhat like a complete skin which another human being could then use while the former occupant returned to phases of inner plane life till he once more contacted in realization his own origins on entry into the Solar Logoidal Sytem—passing once more in reverse back up the path of human evolution as it then was. Such a journey, to which the incarnationary being brought its own experience and added its own quota of development, was much simpler and shorter then than it is now for we are speaking of the beginnings of human history. Now the process is a long and intricate one for after the ending by physical death of a period of development on earth the spirit of man passes on a long journey of inter-incarnationary processes in which the evolutionary phases of the Higher Self are recapitulated again through the previous chains of its development before humanity lived on the present earth. This goes on at the same time that the Personality and higher vehicles recapitulate and absorb in meditation the experiences of the incarnation just ended.

All progress follows the law of recapitulation which involves the great laws of change, transmutation and sacrifice. Physical recapitulation can be observed in the early stages of the human embryo. In the Aquarian Age Yesod is much concerned with redemption and equilibrium.

Note on the inner vehicles of man. In the 'Heroic Age' (and even in later days among the Greek philosophers) the mind did not work in quite the same way as it does today. In the Heroic Age the concrete mind was certainly in use and developing but not nearly so developed as it became later. It followed that the great Archetypes and the Principles behind them worked through the *etheric* body in a manner not possible nowadays. Hence in tales of those days there can be discerned a macrocosmic grandeur in the microcosm. The concrete mind played a relatively smaller part in the make-up of man but the Abstract mind was normally in touch with the 'thinker' of the day. At present the reverse is the case, for the Abstract Mind has receded in the uninitiated generally and it is the destiny of modern man to work as much as may be *through* his concrete mind. Thus everything today is necessarily seen in different perspective. Great heroism indeed does exist today but does not reflect itself, so to speak, *directly* upon the etheric from macrocosmic levels. To the modern mind, for example, the dragging of the body of Hector by Achilles after the latter had slain him seems cruel and dreadful, but it is probable that even the Trojans did not take that view at the time. It was 'gigantic' revenge on the grand scale of Hector and Achilles—a revenge in which the Oversouls of both Greeks and Trojans took part. Thus is drama born or, in Mystery language, thus are rituals built and worked.

The 'Masters' (see also above)

In the East—especially in India—the conditions and atmosphere are much easier to manipulate from the Inner Planes for purposes of manifestation. Such manifestations are of the etheric or subtle aspects of matter and, being of matter, can be termed 'physical' but that word has then a meaning somewhat different from what is usually understood by it. When the Theosophical Society was inaugurated the strongest possible manifestations of the Inner Plane Adepti were needed to impress the teaching, but when that had been achieved the same strength of manifestation was no longer called for.

Concerning the 'incarnations' of Inner Plane Adepti, the question is more complex than usually thought and there are differences between the degrees of incarnation. A suitable disciple of a certain Master can be used by that Master, with the consent and co-operation of the Higher Self of that disciple, for a type of incarnation, and the result would differ little from a genuine incarnation for as long as the Master's purpose required. The incarnating Force, however, would be so incarnated only temporarily and intermittently and the Personality thus manifesting it would not be its own true Projection. An example of this on the very highest level is said to be the manifestation during three years of an aspect of the Christ in the Lord Jesus in order to accomplish a great work, the high initiate who manifested the Force having had other lives on earth directed by his own Spirit.

The Archangel Sandalphon

This Archangel is the guide of the planet Earth—the Regent of Malkuth (see Cosmic Doctrine). He has guided the Earth since Lemurian days and many of his relations with Earth figure in mythologies and the myths of certain gods. His development affects humanity somewhat as the evolution of humanity affects the development of the Earth (the Planetary Spirit as described in the Cosmic Doctrine). The Racial Angels are in his especial jurisdiction and certain countries and their influences are in a deep sense the result of his own stages of growth.

Pallas Athene. Wisdom is virgin and unadulterated. To some extent it is veiled, for the world could not survive the sight of it naked. The deeper into matter it penetrates the more must it be shielded, and therefore it is armed for its own protection: it wears a helmet in order that its own fire shall not destroy the brain; it is begotten, not made; it is born of the Father, i.e. the Divine Spark through Logoidal contact; it bears the spear and holds all knowledge. In short it is Pallas Athene and on her shield is the Gorgon's Head, veiled or unveiled.

PART TWO
ASPECTS OF OCCULTISM

1.

God and the Gods

We are accustomed to think of Christianity, Judaism, and Mohammedanism as the three monotheistic faiths, and all the rest as polytheistic and pagan. But if we look more closely into things we shall find that the most polytheistic religions are at heart monotheistic, and that even the avowedly monotheistic have a certain kinship with polytheism in certain of their aspects.

Monotheism and polytheism are fundamental twin principles representing the one and the many. A religion which has not got a monotheistic basis has never been conceived by the human mind. Even the most primitive animists have some concept of a father of the gods who made heaven and earth and exercises some sort of rule over the innumerable devils of their devotion. The more highly evolved and philosophical a polytheism becomes, the more clearly does it conceive of the One Who creates and dominates the many.

The nearest approach to monotheism that exists is ultra-Protestant Christianity, which has lost its angelology; and even this is a Di-theism, because it worships God the Son as well as God the Father. Concerning God the Holy Ghost, of which it has little understanding, it keeps silence and for all practical purposes ignores It. Catholic Christianity has replaced the gods with the saints, and develops and encourages what is called 'dulia', the veneration paid to minor and specialized manifestations of the divine. The different saints, by virtue of their personal experiences and consequent presumed sympathies, preside over different aspects of human needs and activities. St Christopher is the patron saint of all travellers. There are also local saints, the patrons of localities, to whom pilgrimages are made and prayers are said. What is the difference between this concept and that of the polytheistic Hindu, with his scores of deities, specialized and localized? What is the difference in principle between Ganesa, god of money-lenders, and Christopher, patron saint of travellers?

The only real difference lies in the fact that the instructed Catholic does not pray to the saint as the dispenser of blessings, but implores the saint to intercede for him with Deity. This is a subtle but important point. The uninstructed Catholic, however, makes his prayers and little offerings direct to the saint, troubled by no such fine distinctions; his attitude is exactly the same as that of the uninstructed Hindu. The invocation of a specialized power, believed to be specially appropriate to the occasion, and therefore more efficacious than a generalized beneficence, is deep-rooted in human nature. The out-patient at the hospital scornfully rejects advice on hygiene and demands a bottle of physic, as strongly flavoured and highly coloured as possible.

It is an ineradicable trait in human nature to want something definite and tangible that it can see and handle; St Thomas, the doubting disciple, is the patron saint of many more than those who call upon his name; and be it noted that Our Lord did not express any marked disapproval of his caution, but bid him make his experiment and prove for himself.

It is because of the very nature of our minds that we need this definiteness and tangibility; for our minds are built up by experience of sensory images, and they know no other language. It is only by means of the calisthenics of meditation that the power to conceive abstract ideas is built up, and those less highly developed intellectually never succeed in building it. For them translation into terms of concrete imagery is essential. The One God is for the initiate—the many must have the Many. God must incarnate, must be made man before He can come within range of man's awareness.

The relationship of concept is in many cases a relationship in fact where the more local of the Catholic saints are concerned. A very small amount of archaeological research serves to prove that the local saints are in a very large number of cases local pagan deities, or deities that had important local festivals, which have been taken over, festivals and all, by the Roman Catholic Church when she was organizing her field of missionary activity.

There was great wisdom in this, for local deities and local festivals were a source of income to the neighbourhood, and their abolition would have caused not only local hardship but resistance and rebellion. The wise thing, and the simple thing, in dealing with ignorant folk, was to rechristen the deity and canonize him, and provide him with an appropriate legend. Then the old folk carried on the profitable business of the festival-cum-fair, and the young folk were entertained by the legend, and everybody was happy in their simple way, and in one generation the conversion was effected without inflicting hardship on anybody. The

Roman Catholic Church is a very wise church, and adapts her methods to the nature of the human mind instead of trying to alter human nature from what it is to what it ought to be as a preliminary to salvation.

In the pagan faiths the same principles prevail. The simple soul likes gods and plenty of them, full-flavoured and highly coloured; but the instructed and thoughtful man develops the idea of the God behind the gods, the Creator and Sustainer, Whose nature determines the nature of His creation; right relationship with Whom is essential to man's welfare in this world and the next. This is not a God Who will be satisfied with burnt offerings, but demands a righteous life.

Monotheistic Judaism upon its orthodox side bears much resemblance in spirit to Protestant Christianity, which latter, in actual fact, draws its inspiration from the Old Testament far more than from the New. But mystical Judaism, the Judaism of the Qabalah, knows the Ten Holy Archangels, the spirits before the throne, and innumerable choirs of angels, their servitors. These are the exact analogue of the saints and gods of other faiths. So much so that there exist what are called the tables of correspondences, in which saints, gods, and angels are classified together under their respective headings; and no honest student, with the facts before him, cares to upset that classification, little as it may appeal to a one-way mind, to whom the truth has been delivered once for all in his own little Bethel with the tin roof.

In order to understand a man's point of view we need to put ourself in his place and enter into it imaginatively, even if not sympathetically. We owe a great deal of our misconceptions of other people's faiths to the fact that the first translators of their holy books were in many cases Christian missionaries, and these reserved for the expression of their own teaching all words that had a laudatory meaning, and reserved for the teachings of their opponents, even when these were identical with their own upon specific points, words that had debased associations. If the words that were translated as gods had been translated as archangels, as they ought to have been, we should have had a much better understanding with some of our spiritual neighbours, though of course we might not have contributed so liberally to missionary societies as we have done had we realized that the spiritual plight of these our brethren was by no means desperate.

The different great faiths evolved at different epochs of the world's history and represent different stages of spiritual development. Those who have studied esoteric science know that the different levels of consciousness which correspond to the different planes developed at successive epochs of cosmic evolution. If the great faiths be examined from the standpoint of consciousness—that is to say, from the standpoint of psychology rather than theology, it will be found that they correspond to these different phases of development.

Each religion builds upon the basis left behind by its predecessor, even when it repudiates it and all its works and looks upon its gods as devils. Each religion tries to give a complete answer to the riddle of the Sphinx. But it will be remembered that the riddle of the Sphinx had four clauses, and it is generally to be found that each new faith comes to answer one or another of these clauses and leaves the rest of the problem untouched. Each faith, then, specializes, and at the same time tends to become one-sided.

We shall find that the faith held as the official exoteric religion of his race is the faith that speaks to a man's conscious mind; that his personal religion, if he has any, is the product of his superconscious mind; and that the primitive folk-religion of his race rules over his unconscious mind and fills it with its symbols and images. The racial past lives on in the subconscious mind of each of us, as the Zürich school of psychology recognizes; but it can be evoked to visible appearance in a manner which no orthodox psychologist is acquainted with. It is this evocation of the racial past which is the key to certain forms of ceremonial magic which have as their aim the evocation of Principalities and Powers.

The different gods and goddesses of a polytheistic faith, or the angels and archangels of a monotheistic one, are neither divine creations nor the arbitrary products of the imagination. They are the creations of the created, fashioned in astral substance after a manner well understood by the esotericist, and ensouled by cosmic forces. A cosmic force without an astral form is not a god either. When a cosmic force of a pure type, that is to say, with a single specialized mode of activity, uncontaminated by any alien type of energy to detract from its single-pointedness, is embodied in an astral thought-form of a suitable type, which gives full scope to its activities, we have what is called an artificial Elemental. When the thought-form in which the embodiment takes place is made by the composite efforts of the group-mind of a race, and is ensouled by one of the primary modes of cosmic energy, we have what is called in some faiths a god and in others an archangel.

A god, therefore, is an artificial Elemental of a very powerful type, built up over long periods of time by successive generations whose minds were cast in the same mould. It is therefore a form of such potency that no evocator can hope to dominate it in the way he would an Elemental of his own creating. He must yield himself to its influence and permit it to dominate him if it is to be evoked to visible manifestation. The operator himself is the channel of evocation. It is in his imagination that the image of both god and Elemental builds itself up, and it is the corresponding aspect of his own nature which provides the ensouling force. In the case of an artificial Elemental, however, the whole of the force is derived subjectively; but in the case of a god, objective, racial, cosmic force passes through the corresponding aspect of the operator's nature to ensoul the form.

In the great majority of cases of evocative magic, the form is built up on the astral and can only actually be seen by the clairvoyant, though any sensitive person can feel its influence. It is only when there is a materializing medium as member of the circle that materialization takes place and the form evoked is visible to the physical eye. A tenuous type of form can be induced to build itself up by the use of certain substances that give off ectoplasm, the principal of which is fresh blood; excreta can also be used for the same purpose. A considerable bulk of these unpleasant substances is necessary, however, to get a form of any definiteness, and their virtue is fugitive, for the ectoplasm has gone off by the time the body heat has departed. Therefore for all practical purposes they are of no use to the operator under the ordinary conditions of civilized life; neither can a very high type of presence be induced to manifest through such media. It is necessary to mention them, however, because the fact that they emanate ectoplasm explains certain phenomena of occult pathology. There is also a field of research here for the scientific student with the necessary laboratory equipment, though for obvious reasons it does not lend itself to drawing-room performances or the operations of home circles.

It is valuable to note in this connection that constipation, which is the accumulation of a bulk of excreta within the body, is frequently found to be present in obsessional hallucinations, which yield immediately to the exorcism of a purgative, and it is probable that the accumulation of faeces forms the physical basis of the obsessing entity.

The initiated magician is usually, unless engaged in some special experiment or research, content to evoke to visible appearance on the astral, depending upon his psychic powers for communication with the entity evoked. He does not go to the trouble to evoke to visible appearance on the physical because, if he is an adequate psychic, astral appearance serves his purpose just as well; in fact better, because it is more congenial to the nature of the beings invoked and places less limitation upon their activities.

He knows quite well that it is his own temperament which is the channel of evocation and that his own astral body supplies the basis of manifestation. He knows, therefore, that the chief part of his preparation must be self-preparation. Part of the work of the Mysteries consists in developing grade by grade the different aspects of the microcosm, which is man, and linking them up by means of symbols planted in consciousness with the corresponding macrocosmic aspects, which are the gods. Once a student has taken a given grade, he should be capable of evoking the beings of all grades corresponding to that particular type of cosmic force; and not only of evoking them, for anyone can do that who has a little knowledge and plenty of imagination, but also of controlling their manifestations when evoked. In order to do this he needs to have the corresponding force in himself purified, developed, equilibrated and controlled. His control of the objective manifestation depends entirely on his control of the corresponding subjective factor, or trait in his character. Mars is an easy potency to evoke to visible appearance, but a difficult one to control when evoked; for the control of the Geburah potencies depends entirely upon our control of our own tempers. Equally with Venus, our power over whim depends upon our control of our emotions. To operate in the sphere of Luna we must be very sure of the accuracy of our psychism, which depends upon thought-control.

One of the most important uses of ceremonial working lies in its power to energize any given aspect of our nature, and so bring about a profound change in character, doing in a brief hour's work what years of painful effort and self-discipline might fail to achieve. A man cannot make himself brave by force of will; he can merely keep the outward manifestations of his fear under control, though they may be tearing him to pieces inwardly; but by means of an operation of Mars he may fundamentally change his nature. It is for this reason that ceremonial, and especially talismanic magic is the essential complement of astrology; for astrology is the diagnosis of the trouble, but magic is the treatment of it by means of which the warring forces in our natures are equilibrated.

These things, however, can only be done where there is adequate knowledge, in order that the real needs of a nature may be discerned. It is little use to do an operation of Mars for a person whose fears are not due to lack of courage but to a too lively imagination; an operation of Luna is indicated in such a case. An operation of Mars, misguidedly undertaken, will merely make him excessively quarrelsome.

The karmic record also must be taken into consideration when doing operative magic of a concentrated kind, for some unbalanced manifestations of character may be of the nature of reactions, or what the psychologist calls over-compensations. For instance, the timidity for which an operation of Mars is desired may be due to lack of wisdom in the past which produced disastrous karmic consequences which are even now being worked out. The concentration of a Martial force is not going to help such a condition as that, but will tend to produce fresh problems for it to solve.

Moreover, operations should never come singly, but always in the equilibrating pairs of opposites, and it is usually sound policy to perform the operation of the opposite Pillar previous to the performance of the operation whose effect is specifically desired. For instance, if the energizing effects of Mars (Geburah, Severity) are desired, it would be highly desirable to perform a few days previously an operation of Jupiter (Chesed, Mercy) which balances Mars in the opposite column of the Tree of Life when the symbols are set up according to the system of the Qabalists. If this is done, all the good of Mars will be obtained without any of the evil of its unbalanced influence.

Although the highly concentrated form of a force should only be applied by an expert to one who has undergone the necessary preparation leading up thereto, there can be little doubt that life could be made much richer, and our temperaments far more vital and equilibrated were we to observe the times and seasons in a way that all primitive faiths that are in close touch with nature observe them. The Catholic aspect of the Christian faith, which is its most occult aspect, scrupulously observes the seasons of the Christian year, which is really a sun-worship year; but the Protestant aspect has no realization whatsoever of what it is doing, and drags itself through the fifty-two Sundays with one set of altar-frontals and a plain white surplice.

The Four Elements, the seven planets, and the twelve signs of the Zodiac are prime factors of the cosmos. Each of these has its tide and season of ascendency, and each has its appropriate symbols and rites developed in one or another of the great pagan systems of nature worship. Nature worship be it noted, is not idolatry, but the adoration of God made manifest in nature, and is an exceedingly important aspect of both our faith and our psychology, though one but little understood in the Christian system and Western countries.

The different gods and archangels of the different systems, Egyptian,

Greek, Chaldean, Norse, which are native to our culture, are the racial thought-forms built up to act as vehicles of these primary cosmic forces. Being the primitive faith of our racial culture, their symbols lie deep hidden in the subconscious mind of each of us, utterly ineradicable, and capable of evocation to conscious activity by the use of the appropriate means.

All the pagan pantheons contain the same factors because they all have to minister to the needs of a human nature that does not vary very much as to its ingredients from race to race and age to age, but merely in the proportion in which these are on the average compounded: The north has more head and the south more heart; the east more intuition and the west more will; but neither head nor heart are entirely absent from any race on the earth's surface. Systems, consequently, are built up and specialized according to the temperament of the people they minister to.

Consequently, when we want to perform a rite of any given type we find it convenient to choose a method which is most closely fitted to the needs of the moment and our own temperamental bias.

The Chaldean magic of the Qabalah appeals to those who are imbued with a strict monotheism and regard all objects of adoration with unfamiliar names as devils. Egyptian magic appeals to those who are metaphysically minded, and Greek Mystery methods to the artistic, because the Greek invocations depend upon music and movement for their efficacy.

These three systems form the primary basis of our Western Tradition; they also represent its most highly developed aspects. But for all practical purposes they present many difficulties in the employment, and people who try them usually get only partial effects unless they are very advanced workers, or have a special natural aptitude and affinity for the particular tradition according to which they are operating.

The reason for this is not far to seek. None of these methods has been naturalized in our islands, and we cannot therefore find a holy place at which to pick up the contacts in a prepared atmosphere where the veil is thin and the foot of Jacob's ladder rests upon earth. Moreover, the racial subconsciousness, although it contains all the elements represented by the exotic gods and goddesses (for we are not made of special and peculiar clay, different from the rest of mankind), does not contain the symbols that evoke them in the form in which they have been built up in the racial subconsciousness of the races that were habituated to their daily use as objects of adoration. It is only because these races are dead and gone and their cultures have passed away that we can use their symbols at all; for if the system were a living system, it would automatically exclude us from its penetralia unless right of entry had been conferred upon us. It is for this reason that we can never operate a living system of magic effectually unless its degrees have been conferred upon us. The Voodoo and the Tantric systems are closed systems to the European, but the Egyptian and the Chaldean are open systems, which anyone may operate who can, because their priests are dead and their temples stand open to sun and wind and there is no one to guard their mysteries from profanation save the intrinsic powers of those mysteries themselves. These, however, are a quite effectual guard for all practical purposes, for though they cannot prevent the blasphemer from having his first bite, as it were, he seldom has a second, for the powers he has evoked and profaned destroy him.

But why should we esteem an outraged deity a devil? Because a misused force reacts on the user, it is not necessarily a force of evil. Has no one ever taken a poisonous overdose of a drug? Or received a shock when he touched the wrong switch? Or miscalculated the temperature of an object and burnt his fingers? If we banished from human use as dangerous every object or substance that had ever under any circumstances proved noxious, we should exist in a vacuum.

These powers, however, duly approached with reverence and understanding, and after the purification demanded for their worship, can still exert their ancient influence over the worshipper, blessing and illuminating him according to their nature and his capacity for response.

These great potencies, thus approached, have infinite possibilities for good to exercise upon human consciousness and social life; and especially is this the case in our modern urban civilization where the nature contacts have been lost and forgotten, and in consequence the subconscious minds of men and women are as foul as uncleansed stables. We need the light and air of conscious attention to be directed to our subconscious fastnesses, and the clean broom of spiritual sanctification to make a clean sweep of their accumulated rubbish and refuse. There is nothing in human nature which is intrinsically unclean, St Augustine notwithstanding, but there is a very great amount which will go septic and putrefy if we thrust it below the level of consciousness and sit upon the lid. It is a false concept of human nature which has developed so much that is worst in human nature.

When we deny the natural side of our natures, we are like a woman who will not clean a stopped sink because it is too dirty to touch. It may be unpleasant to handle when first it is taken in hand and cleared up, but once clean, it need never be allowed to get into that condition again; but it will certainly be a source of poison to the whole household until it is taken in hand.

The pagans were right when they deified and sanctified all aspects of nature and of human nature. The Romans even adored Cloaca, the goddess of sewers and scavengers, and they were far cleaner and more sanitary in their habits than the generations who succeeded them, and whose saints refrained from washing out of love for God.

We need to bring back reverence for natural things, and respect for the body and its functions, and adore God made manifest in nature, even in the form of the goddess Cloaca, if we are to have any real health of mind, body or estate, and return as prodigals to the bosom of our Great Mother, where alone is to be found healing for the diseases that arise from too much civilization and too little sun and air.

2.

Sacred Centres

'. . . For lead and tin are not produced from the earth . . . It is a fountain that produces them, and an angel stands therein.'

BOOK OF ENOCH.

I don't think that it will be disputed that certain places exert a powerful influence on human beings.

Egypt seems to be the best known one, for most people return from there having had an experience of some kind. It is said that this is caused by the electricity generated by the ever-moving sands of the great Sahara desert, which so changes the normal rate of vibration, that an extension of consciousness is the result. This must naturally depend on the individual; a purely material person would be affected in a very different way from one who is psychic. Unfortunately we are seldom given the ordinary man's experience, which might, in many cases, be of more interest and use to humanity than the vague visionings of the psychically inclined.

In every country there are these centres, but unfortunately, since the Christian era, they have been appropriated by the Church; and some of the most vital have been prefixed by the title of 'Saint', when perhaps the influence exerted might not be at all of a saintly character. Thus, the old name, that might have given a clue to the particular influence, is submerged, and in this way much of the ancient lore is lost, because the Church recognizes only one kind of experience—that of the purely religious ecstasy, which is the most emotional and primitive, and therefore to the ordinary mind, the most wonderful, for it is a state of intoxication, and is therefore a purely selfish and personal experience, entirely to do with individual development along a particular line, and from the physical point of view is nearly always abortive because undirected. I emphasize the physical effect, because what its mysteries are on another plane, or state of consciousness, one can only dimly sense, or understand the effect on the journeyings of the soul.

There is little, if any, guidance given by the Church to those who open these doors, for it is not given to all to experience the higher religious emotion; and instead of a readjustment of values—a further vision or extension of consciousness and a breaking through some of the veils of matter—the effect is, as I have said, abortive, for the experience is so shattering to the untrained and unprepared mind, that it disturbs the normal outlook on life.

There is also another side to these experiences, and of this we hear but little. Those who enter the dark portals which lead to the dread subterranean palaces of Qliphoth, and whose way is no longer that of the normal individual, return from this journey with their bias towards evil intensified.

In the Mystery Schools each initiate was carefully watched and guided, so that the experience should not be lost or allowed to destroy instead of to reconstruct. We go to these places, and are not told *what* kind of experience to expect, beyond that it will be of a religious order, or contact with nature (a vague term) and therefore we go in a negative condition of mind, with will and intellect unprepared, and so the real value is completely lost in an emotional storm.

As I said before, I believe that in the old names lie the secret of the influence exerted, and these have to do with the physical, or rather the contact that lies deep in the earth.

In the magical writings we read that each metal has its particular planet, that each human being is under the influence of a planet; and it may be that a scientific fact lies in this statement which in the future will be explained in scientific language by scientific men.

During the eclipse of the sun in 1928, some experiments were made by a Dr Kolisko with solutions of gold, silver, lead, and tin; pictures that were taken of these before, during, and after the eclipse showed remarkable changes in activity, indicating that the celestial phenomenon had an effect, and a very marked one on these solutions.

It would be interesting to study geologically these centres, their ancient names and qualities, apart from those attributed to them by the Church, and see if we could get at the particular energizing force, and so direct it consciously to our purpose.

By working along these lines man could co-operate with the celestial powers who have their physical focuses in the earth, and so gain much in health, power, and intellect.

In every country is the Head and Heart centre, or shall we say the

Spiritual centre, and these are linked to similar centres in other countries, and sometimes form interesting diagrams. We can all spot the Head centre for that is naturally the capital of the country, but the Heart or Spiritual centre is more obscure and only known to comparatively few. It is quite possible that in a country there may be as many centres as there are in a human body, for a country has a definite life and soul of its own.

Just to give an example on purely religious lines: The great cathedrals of England—Durham, Chester, Lincoln, Wells, Winchester, and Canterbury form the double triangle or hexagram, but these centres are very old, and were the sites of pagan temples in pre-Christian times, and to recover the type of influence one would have to seek their old names or meaning of the names. Such diverse sites cannot all exert the same influence fundamentally, though it is possible that those only in tune to Christian influences and going no deeper than that level, might only contact that particular vibration.

The mineral and metallic world is the oldest and densest, and in it must lie many secrets; could we contact its consciousness much might be recovered for the benefit of mankind.

That the ancient Druids knew of the connection of planetary with physical matter is proved by their circles. In the south of England, taking Silbury Hill as the Earth, they have worked out correctly the orbs of the planets in relation to it. The orbit of Venus is contained in the circle of stones at Winterbourne Basset; the temples of the Sun and Moon are just north of the hill, the orbit of the Sun encircling it. The orbit of Mars is at Marsden; the orbit of Mercury at Walken Hill; of Jupiter at Casterly Camp, and that of Saturn at Stonehenge. There are also the seven churches in Ireland; the five churches of Stowting, Kent (though tradition tells of seven), and there are many others. These were all pagan temples.

When St Augustine wrote in AD 597 to Pope Gregory for advice concerning the many pagan places of worship he found, the answer he received was—'To use them when possible, in order that the people may the more familiarly resort to the places to which they have been accustomed'.

All over the United Kingdom are these places, for the Druids built nothing without knowledge, and one hopes that an endeavour will be made to recover their ancient wisdom, the proof of which is so ably put forth in Mr Lewis Spense's *Mysteries of Britain*.

I am convinced that they had some method of contacting the great subconscious of the world, where the Past, Present, and Future lie ready to be unfolded. That their training was a long and arduous one is certain, for that an ordered training does develop powers latent in everyone is proved by those who have been fortunate enough to be in touch with a teacher who is also an initiate and initiator; but I am sure that not only the teacher, but the time and place are to be taken into account.

We walk in this wonderful world of ours as if we were not of it, but a creation apart; but we are the world, and have within our bodies every part of it, and therefore must be affected by all that concerns it. The magnetic qualities of its stone and mass of metals, the generating life of animal and vegetable nature, all play their part, but could we bring our intellect to help us, I feel sure that we could attain a result beyond our expectations.

The magician of old had to work in secret for he was more or less an outcast, unless he allied himself with others such as the Druid did, and later the Rosicrucians, so forming a strong body.

The modern magician specializes and is a freelance—men like those who have attained such tremendous speed in the air, doctors. and men of science with their microscopes and electrical appliances. All these are trained occultists, and far on the path to Adeptship. They are highly trained specialists and efficient parts of a whole, which, united will bring to us knowledge of the world we live in, for they have reached an extension of consciousness far beyond that of the ordinary man, and their training has been as hard as, if not harder, than that of their predecessors of old.

Sacred Centres II

'Other sheep have I that are not of this fold.'

JOHN X. 16

There are many planes interpenetrating our world, inhabited by beings like, and yet unlike, ourselves, invisible and unknown to each other and to man. This is due to their different rates of vibration. I will give a very crude example—that of the electric fan. When revolving slowly, its propellers are seen distinctly, increase its rate and nothing is seen but a blur.

This example only holds with regard to one sense, namely that of sight, but intensify and extend to all senses in an ascending and descending scale, and we could imagine how several cycles of life could, at the same time, occupy the same space, unknown to each other.

That will also show the reason why different people have such diverse experiences at the same place, and in psychometry, with the same object.

We all have our own particular rate of vibration, so that every one of us must be in close tune with one at least of these elemental ratios, and it is possible that the day may come, indeed may not be so very far distant, when by an act of will we shall be able to change our own ratio to that of whatever cycle of life we wish to contact. That such a thing will be possible in the future is foreshadowed in an article by Professor Low, where he says in regard to telepathy that 'Thought is an electrical process and must be capable of transmission; it may be centuries before we are able to effect the transmission . . . but it is certainly bound to come.' In the future we may actually, and with all our senses, be aware of these denizens of a hitherto unknown and invisible world.

It is unlikely that man should be the only form of life to be attracted to the source of energy that is generated in these places, but that other beings would also, and for the same reason, seek them.

There are in this world many tides of varying length, which are called in Eastern terminology 'Tattvas', and these range in length from thousands of years to a few minutes. The greater ones we are only aware of by looking back on the rise and fall of civilizations and the changes on the face of the globe. These are under the dominion of one of the great Northern Constellations, but there are many lesser ones, and to these we can attribute the falling into disuse of some of our centres, and the gradual reopening of others. In the last hundred years or so there has been the uncovering of many buried cities and even great civilizations with their many Gods and creeds.

Whenever a place has had prayers and concentrated desires directed towards it, it forms an electrical vortex that gathers to itself a force, and it is for a time a coherent body that can be felt and used by man. It is round these bodies of force that shrines, temples, and in later days churches are built; they are the Cups that receive the Cosmic downpouring focused on each particular place.

There is very little teaching on these matters, and I think it advisable now to speak of the dangers that may be encountered from the *lesser known and more primitive psychic centres*. That there was a danger was recognized by the Druids and Romans, for they raised altars and offered sacrifices to these woodland peoples, and it was an act of propitiation, for if *you* don't give, *they* take, and what they take is unfortunately something that you cannot spare. It is life-force, for they seek ever to come closer to man, to mingle with him and to take on his ratio, for it is said therein lies their hope of immortality.

Should we wish to help these 'Sheep of another fold', we can do so by a wish to understand their needs and by bringing to them a knowledge of the finer ideals of our later times, and in that way the sacrifice need not be one that is hurtful to our health and sanity.

We must remember, however, that they are of an older and more elemental race, that they belong to another country, and that their laws are quite different, so that we might be seriously injured in mind and body by such encounters, for our bodies are not adapted to bear the brunt of the violent impact of those who differ in almost every way from ourselves.

It is said that there are fairy marriages; these can only happen between those whose ratio is the same, but therein generally lies sadness and heartbreak, unless entered into with understanding.

Pan and his fellows are still to be seen and heard, though these encounters are not so spectacular as story would have us believe, and are generally disagreeable and frightening, and not to be encouraged or wished for. We may enter these unknown regions lightheartedly, but to get away from them and rid oneself of unpleasant attachments is not easy, and help is not always at hand when required.

3.

Christianity and Reincarnation

Why is it that there is no teaching concerning Reincarnation in the Christian doctrine? Is there not even an implied denial of this fundamental doctrine of esoteric philosophy? These questions are frequently asked, and it is exceedingly important that they should be satisfactorily answered if our claim that Christianity is a Mystery religion is to be justified. If we cannot show that the doctrine of reincarnation, so fundamental to esoteric science, is not only not antagonistic to Christ's teaching, but actually implicit therein, we shall be obliged to admit that no Christian can be an occultist and no occultist a Christian.

The doctrine of reincarnation has been lost to European thought since the days of ancient Greece, when it was taught in the Mystery Schools under the name of Metempsychosis and profoundly influenced the outlook of Grecian thinkers. It was also a fundamental doctrine of both the Gnostics and Neo-platonists, and formed an integral part of the attempted blend of the Ancient Wisdom and the New Revelation.

The Mystery Schools in the days of the early Church were open to grave objection. They had fallen upon decadence; phallic rites, blood sacrifices, and black magic generally had crept into them, and though no doubt there were individual groups of initiates who retained their purity, the movement as a whole was justifiably suspect. Christianity spread at first among unlettered folk, and these, already imbued with decent men's horror of the decadence of the popular religion, unable from lack of letters to understand the viewpoint of the philosophers, condemned all learning as of the devil because so many of the learned had given themselves over to evil. Thus it came about that the rise of Christianity saw the decline of learning, and although the worst of the pagan vices were undoubtedly swept away with the abolition of the corrupt religions, yet if we are honest we must admit that these vices were not inherent in paganism but in human nature, and that the abolition of the ancient faiths has not abolished human frailty.

There came about a divorce between learning and religion; metaphysics was abandoned to the philosophers, and the Christian concerned himself with ethics and a dogmatic theology based upon an interpretation of the Sacred Scriptures to which certain keys were lacking—the key of the Qabalah, possessed by the writers of the Old Testament books, and the key of the Gnosis, possessed by the writers of the New Testament books. In consequence, many of the technical terms of the philosophy of both these Mystery Schools have passed unrecognized and been so gravely mistranslated that they have been completely wrested from their meaning, and whole passages perverted or rendered incomprehensible. Would that there were a translation of the Scriptures by an initiate!

The gulf between Christianity and philosophy became wider when the Emperor Constantine made use of the Church for political purposes. Men were placed in high positions whose qualifications lay in their political views rather than their spiritual vision. Its lofty mystical spirit was lost to the Church as well as its metaphysics. The Dark Ages ran their gloomy course, and it was not until the Renaissance came to free and inspire the human spirit that mysticism again lifted its head in the Christian fold.

With the Renaissance came a sudden day-spring of activity in every department of human life after the long inertia of the Dark Ages; but the connecting-link with the Mystery Schools had been broken, and when men came to the study of the ancient philosophers, they approached them from without the gate, not from within. These philosophers, were, to a man, initiates of one school or another of the Mysteries, and they used the technicalities of those rites. Without this key their writings are largely incomprehensible. Uninitiated students, trying to deal with the ancient philosophers by the light of pure scholarship, are in the position of a modern intelligent reader who tries to master a text-book of physics without any previous acquaintance with mathematics. Many of the technical terms employed will be familiar to him, but he will understand them in their popular, not their technical sense, and will be unable to follow the argument.

European thought, raising its battered head after the Renaissance, knew nothing of the Mystery teaching, and the doctrine of reincarnation was lost to Europe with the fall of the classical civilization.

But the inner spiritual life of the soul went on; and whether it is behind convent walls, or in the illuminations of Jacob Böhme and other orthodox mystics, knowledge of the Unseen and its powers was recovered piecemeal by direct revelation. What secret knowledge is guarded within the innermost circle of the Roman Catholic Church today, those outside that circle do not know; they can only judge by the 'signs following'; what mystical illuminations follow upon the silent meditations and fervent prayers of the encloistered orders of Christendom are seldom told.

It may be of interest in this respect to quote from a letter which was sent by the great Cardinal Mercier, the scholarly Archbishop of Malines, to Professor Lutoslavski, the Polish philosopher, in answer to his query as to the ruling of the Roman Church concerning the doctrine of reincarnation, in which he states that 'the doctrine of reincarnation has never been formally condemned by the Roman Church as heretical.'

The exoteric Church of Christ may have forgotten reincarnation, and ceased to teach it, but when reminded of it, it does not condemn it.

If reincarnation is such an important part of the Mystery teaching, from which it is claimed that all religions take their rise, why was it that Our Lord did not teach it explicitly? The explanation of this problem is two-fold; firstly, it lies in the nature of the people to whom He came, and secondly, in the manner in which His work had to be carried out.

Our Lord came to a people, the great majority of whom were exclusively preoccupied, as far as their religious life was concerned, with the formal observances of the Temple and the righteousness inculcated by the Mosaic Law. Among these people were a small minority who were interested in mystical speculations. Of these the most notable body were the Essenes—men and women highly respected in Israel, some of whom lived community lives while others shared in the life of the world. They might not inaptly be called the Quakers of Judaism. The doctrine of reincarnation was part of the teaching of the Essenes, and an important part. It is believed by many that the boy Jesus was educated in an Essenian community after His greatness had been recognized by the elders when He taught in the Temple. Schure, in his very interesting book, *The Great Initiates*, has gathered together the evidence in support of this view.

In all His teaching Our Lord makes a clear distinction between that which He would say to His chosen and trusted disciples in the Upper Chamber, to whom it was given to know the Mysteries of the Kingdom, and the populace whose sick He healed and whose sorrows He comforted.

Our Lord stood forth against a mystical background; He spoke as one coming from behind the Veil. The modern divine knows very little about the ancient mysticism of Israel, the Qabalah; but the Qabalah is the key to the mystical interpretation of the Old Testament and of many passages in the New Testament. Take for instance the closing passage of the Lord's Prayer, 'For thine is the kingdom, the power, and the glory, for ever and ever. Amen.' What does this convey to the Qabalist? A picture of the lower triangle of the Sephirothic Tree of Life, whereon in their appointed pattern are ranged the mystical stations of the Ten Divine Emanations that formed the worlds—Netzach, victory or power; Hod, glory; Malkuth, the kingdom. On the Tree of Life is based the mighty invocation of Qabalistic magic with which every magus seals his aura before commencing any magical operation, 'A teh Malkuth, ve Gedulah, ve Geburah, le Olahm. Amen.' 'For to Thee is the kingdom, and the power and the glory, to the ages, Amen.'

No one can hope to understand Christianity who does not understand the mysticism of the Qabalah in which the above quotation proves that Our Lord was trained, and in the Qabalistic doctrine we shall find among its most important tenets, that of reincarnation.

It is in the Qabalah we find the cosmology and mystical doctrine of the soul and its iniation in which exoteric Christianity is so lamentably weak as compared with the great Eastern faiths. An abundance of esoteric material can be found in both the Old and the New Testament; and what there was before it underwent editing at the hands of generations of scholars who were Churchmen first and last, who can say?

There are many teachings of Our Lord, many passages of Scripture which can only be understood in the light of the doctrine of reincarnation. John the Baptist's message to Jesus is a case in point. Our Lord taught to His disciples in the Upper Chamber a doctrine of which we have no direct record, but many echoes.

From the esoteric point of view it is readily seen why Our Lord did not stress the doctrine of reincarnation in His mission. Each Christos Who comes to the world has a special mission to fulfil in relation to the evolution of humanity. Osiris taught his people the arts of civilization, Krishna taught them philosophy, Buddha taught the way of escape from the bondage of matter, Abdul Baha taught social morality. If there are those who object to these Great Ones being ranked with Our Lord as manifestations of God and Saviours of mankind, then esoteric science must agree to differ from them, for it has always taught that all these be brethren, the Elder Sons of God, showing forth His Glory in human form for the guidance of mankind. On the other hand, initiates of the Western Tradition will not agree to Our Lord being swept aside as merely a good man who taught according to his lights, nor yet a medium who was used by the Christ. The anti-Christian bias of Mme Blavatsky is regrettable, for it has led to a belittling of Christianity among students of occultism which is not justified by the facts and leads to disastrous results in practice.

No man who reads history without prejudice can escape from the fact that there has never been any truth once for all delivered to mankind. This doctrine went its way together with the catastrophic concept of geology. It is the doctrine of evolution alone which has stood the tests of time and facts, and we shall be wise if we accept the conclusion that the law of evolution applies to the spiritual life of mankind as well as its physical life.

Our Lord built upon the foundation of His predecessors, and brought to the Temple His own specific contribution. He had a particular task to do in the cosmic polity, and He is called in the Mysteries the Lord of the Personality.

The older faiths, which also had their Divine Founders, each had for their task the development and illumination of a different layer of consciousness. The very primitive cults, such as Voodooism, were initiators of the sub-consciousness; loftier cults, such as Hinduism, were initiators of the Higher Self; Our Lord's task was to bring regeneration within reach of the common man and to initiate the Personality, using that word in its technical esoteric sense as the aspect of consciousness which is built up out of the experiences that fall to our lot between birth and death. It was this lower, temporal self that He had to bring into line with spiritual life, and link up with the eternal Self.

This lower self is not immortal. No one who is adequately instructed in esoteric philosophy believes in the reincarnation of the present personality, nor of any historic personality in the past. It is the Higher Self alone which is immortal and which survives bodily death and is the vehicle of Karma. Our Lord therefore, having for His task as Saviour to His epoch the making of a Way of Salvation for the personality, naturally did not teach reincarnation as part of His mission because it does not apply to the personality.

The illuminati of His epoch knew this doctrine, whether they were the Essenian mystics of Israel or the initiates of the Greek or Egyptian Mysteries. They needed no instruction on this point, being already familiar with it. But the common man needed to be told that he was the son of God and that God loved him, for this was a thing that had never been known to the world before.

It has been said that Our Lord was well content to allow the doctrine of reincarnation to be forgotten during His epoch because when over-stressed, it is productive of much evil, for it tends to inculcate a *laissez faire* which is disastrous to human progress. The results of the universal acceptance of the doctrine of reincarnation with all its implications are shown in the pages of Katharine Mayo's much discussed book, *Mother India*. Europeans, eating, drinking and making merry because tomorrow they may die, taught of their philosophy to seize the passing day, have become habituated to a remorseless drive of life which has accomplished most of the world's work to date. The doctrine of reincarnation is the most illuminating of teaching when rightly understood, but it is a disastrous doctrine for the ignorant, for unless it is used as a means of evolution, it becomes a folding of the hands in sleep, and bankruptcy of all physical things comes as a thief in the night.

To sum up, the esoteric attitude concerning the doctrine of reincarnation in Christianity may be defined as follows. Reincarnation was part of the Mystery teaching of Israel of which Our Lord and His inner group of disciples were initiates. It was part of the inner teaching of the Christian faith until mysticism became divorced from orthodoxy. It is not repudiated by the Roman Catholic Church. Our Lord did not enlarge upon the doctrine of reincarnation in His public mission because that mission concerned the salvation of the Personality, which does not reincarnate.

4.

The Astral Plane

The Astral Plane has very rightly been called the Plane of Illusion, for people have such varied ideas concerning it. In studying the technique of the planes one may fall into the error of regarding them only as separate and distinct modes of consciousness; whereas, on closer consideration we shall see that they are interrelated and actually function in pairs.

The words 'Kill out desire', as translated by H. P. Blavatsky in *The Voice of the Silence*, are frequently misinterpreted to mean that the Astral Plane, which correlates with desire and emotion, shall be inhibited from function as far as is practicable. Taking, however, the full context of that teaching it is evident that the killing out of desire is a very lofty ideal of the soul when it shall have risen above the planes of the Personality, but while functioning on the mundane plane in the physical senses, we must first kill out the desire for vice and use the forces of emotion and desire for good purpose. It is this point of view that I wish to put before you.

Much of the information concerning the Astral Plane is gathered from psychics and spiritualistic sources with varying degrees of reliability, but the teaching I am giving here has come to us from a Master of the Inner Planes.

'Do you understand the purpose of the plane of illusion? (the astral plane). It serves more purposes than working out the frustration of desires. It is the plane of the manifestation of power for the physical plane. You need to realize that the astral plane is a plane of 'force' and the physical plane is a plane of 'form'. That gives you the clue to a great deal if you think out its implications.

'Do you realize that there is no force on the physical plane and no form on the astral? Do you further realize that a thought-form is a correct description? Then you will see that the cube of manifestation falls into two divisions—the physical half and the mental half and the astral plane divides them. One half having mind for a background and one half matter for a background. You may conceive, therefore, two planes of form with a plane of force connecting them. And you have, therefore, the 'three' which is essential for function—the positive 'form' of mind and the negative 'form' of matter, and the emotional 'force' flowing and returning which connects them.'

Perhaps this will be clearer if we tabulate it thus:

SPIRITUAL PLANE	—	Force
MENTAL PLANE	—	Form
ASTRAL PLANE	—	Force
PHYSICAL PLANE	—	Form

We are taught that duality is necessary for manifestation, and we see here the duality of form and force which are essential to manifestation. Therefore we must consider the astral forces in relation to physical and mental forms.

We are also accustomed to regard the laws of polarity as on one plane—horizontal, but the esoteric teachings show that the same principle may be applied vertically, and the mental, positive stimulus may polarize with the physical, negative aspect, and that the astral forces ensouling those forms with life complete the trinity of function. (This may be better understood by students of the Qabalistic *Tree of Life*, where we have the side pillars in polarity and the central pillar representing the flow of Life forces direct.)

'Now what you want to realize is this—that there is upon that plane of pure force a population of forms which do not derive from that plane at all. They derive firstly in evolutionary order from the plane of mind. Pure mind supplies the first thought-forms, and these forms, being in relation to feelings, serve as vehicles of expression for the feelings. They are all symbolic and geometrical in form. These are the primary forms of the astral. They are the oldest and the highest and the purest form-types. They are the bases of physical form.

'Then, in contradistinction to these, are those astral forms which are evolved in consciousness out of physical sensation. They have matter for a background.

'If you want to understand the astral plane, think of the true astral plane as consisting of streaming rays of light without form at all, and the 'forms' of the astral, whether derived from mind or matter, as distinct from the pure emotional forces as are the human beings from the land they walk about on. You have, therefore, the plane and its inhabitants.

'Now the inhabitants of the astral plane are creatures of the mind. The life and function of the astral goes on behind them and through them, but it is not they. The astral thought-form is a creation of the mind, whether it be a primary creation of mind working direct on emotions, or whether it be a secondary creation of mind working on emotions stimulated by sensation (physical).

'The ordinary untrained human mind functions only when stimulated by sensation, therefore all its thoughts are determined by the nature of the sensation which stimulates them. But the mind of the occultist knows that the primary form is the mental form, and it can make those forms independently of physical sensation. A form on the astral plane acts as a channel for and determines the configuration of the astral forces, and therefore all manifestations of force in matter depend upon the astral thought-form and are determined by it.

'Matter adheres to type because the forces function through thought-forms derived from matter. So that matter gives rise to the form and the form to matter in a never-ending and stereotyped circle. It is fixed and defined. But although no variation can take place from the plane of matter, variation is possible from the plane of mind; and if a new thought-form be created on the astral, a new form would appear on the physical. The physical form will give rise to the appropriate sensation, and the sensation will reinforce the thought-form, and so the cycle will become stereotyped in its turn.

'You have, then, the thought-form on the astral and the physical form on the material plane—soul and body—of whatever object, or organism, or organization, or happenings may be under consideration. You have, in fact, the cause and the effect. The astral cause giving rise to the physical effect, and the physical effect re-creating the astral cause. You will realize from this that the forms of the astral are all mental images, and some are the product of sensation, and some are the product of imagination. It is by availing yourself of the powers of the image-forming faculties of the mind that you can set the astral causes in motion. Whatever image you can make in the imagination—provided it be in accordance with Cosmic Law and therefore possible of manifestation—if you make it sufficiently clearly in all its parts to have a workable mechanism, and if you hold it long enough and steadily enough and pour in the force of the will strongly enough—will come to pass on the physical plane in manifestation, or upon whatever plane it shall be directed to.

'But in all your making, remember this—that you will have to face the consequences of your creation whatever it may be; and good intentions will not protect you from the results of an error of judgment; and when you elect to use the powers of the human mind you take risks. But remember also this—that those who serve God always take risks because they know them to be worth taking. And the expression of the Logoidal Mind can only be brought through into the plane of manifestation by those who are prepared to take the risk of endeavouring to perceive the abstract and concrete it as best they may.

'The spiritual forces cannot work themselves out on the plane of form now that the form is so highly organized, without the use of intermediaries, and so some have to be found who will take the risk of endeavouring, with the finite consciousness, to discern the Mind of God and to express it on the planes of form.'

There is an interesting corroboration of the intermediaries who work out the Mind of God on its passage from Spirit to Matter in the Communications received from the astral plane by the Revd G. Vale Owen, which has reference to the co-operation of thought and emotion:

'No emotion no thought, here is without its outer manifestation. All you see around you from your place upon the earth is the manifestation of thought . . . The Source of all thought is He from Whom it proceeds and to Whom it returns in a never-ending cycle.

'Between times this thought-stream passes through the mentality of personalities of varying degrees of authority, and also of loyalty or oneness with Him. This thought-stream, passing through these Princes, Archangels, Angels, and Spirits, becomes manifest through them externally in Heavens, Hells, Constellations of Suns, Sun-Systems, Races, Nations, Animals, Plants, and all those entities which you call things.

'All these come into existence by means of persons thinking from themselves outward, when their thoughts take on expression, tangible to the senses of those who inhabit the sphere in which the thinkers dwell or with which they are in touch.'

'To resume the teaching, the following remarks on the difficult subject of astral shells are illuminating:

'When the time comes for the initiate to claim his freedom from incarnation, he asks for and obtains the task of concreting the Cosmic idea. If, as very rarely happens, he succeeds in concreting it perfectly, he is not destroyed by it, but undergoes that liberation which is known in Christian theology as translation. "He walks with God and is not." But if, as more often happens, he does but bring a contribution to the building of the Temple, the imperfection of the work destroys him. That is to say, it breaks up the personality.

'Now the Individuality which has a Personality broken in this way, is karma free, because when a Personality is thus shattered by the Cosmic forces, death on all the planes takes place simultaneously, and there is therefore no karma. All that is left to the immortal spirit is the mental picture which is sometimes called the seed-atom of the concrete. That mental picture abides in the atmosphere of the upper astral or the akashic records and is the sole link between the spirit and the plane of form. The spirit then has for its vehicle the abstract mind stored with the garnered riches of the evolution of that entity. It has also the simulacrum on the astral, but that simulacrum is only the shadow it threw in the past on the plane of form.

'The entity that elects to function in relation to the advancement of the human race galvanizes that simulacrum into a transient life in order to communicate with those whose consciousnesses cannot rise above forms. When once the consciousness of a human being has become aware of the galvanized simulacrum, the same cycle of cause and effect as that already described takes place in his consciousness until his imagination builds up a clear image of the Master, and into that image the powers of that entity flow and function.

'The difference between the man who touches astral imagination only and the man who, by astral imagination touch spiritual actualities, is that the former in his concepts can rise no higher than the astral imagination, and the latter has in his soul spiritual realization and aspiration which he brings through into brain consciousness by means of the astral imagination.'

From these teachings it will be seen how important the astral plane is. When we think, we create astral images, and when in meditation we seek inspiration, it comes through astral imagination.

There are other and more subconscious ways in which the astral forces work; for instance—in deep sleep when consciousness is dissociated from the physical senses, the body will be recuperated by astral power. The physical-etheric body is fed, as it were, by the astral forces, and the astral force is controlled by the 'form' aspect of the mental body, for without 'form' the astral would be diffused and without function. The earth, sun, moon, vegetation and all life-forces which derive from the One Source of Life—God—have their astral aspect and reach us through the etheric body. We must therefore learn to give proper value to the astral plane and not strive to repress its power, for if we do, those powers may flow forth into various conditions of astral pathologies, and have their physical reaction.

The forces of the lower astral plane are directed towards the personal and physical well-being, whereas the forces of the upper astral state of consciousness, with their aspiration and uplifting powers, have a background of universal well-being. A healthy astral condition manifests itself on the physical plane in orderliness, good-feeling, love of art, music and things that appeal to the better feelings; and unhealthy astral conditions will open the door to undesirable contacts arising from unworthy thoughts and desires, dirt and disorder.

Death does not change our astral consciousness, for we are assured that what we are now, so shall we be when we awaken on the astral plane free from the limitations of the physical senses. Let us then prepare for that state here and now, so that by realization we shall hasten our progress towards the spiritual goal which we can only reach by way of the astral plane.

5.

The Worship of Isis

All the gods are one god; and all the goddesses are one goddess, and there is one initiator.

In the beginning was space and darkness and stillness, older than time and forgotten of the gods. Movement arose in space: that was the beginning.

This sea of infinite space was the source of all being; life arose therein as a tide in the soundless sea. All shall return thereto when the night of the gods draws in. This is the Great Sea, Marah, the Bitter One; the Great Mother. And because of the inertia of space ere movement arose as a tide, She is called by the Wise the Passive Principle in Nature and is thought of as Water, or Space that Flows. But there is no flowing in space till the power stirs; and this power is the Active Principle of creation. All things partake of the nature of the Active or the Passive Principle, and are referred thereto.

Thrice-greatest Hermes graved on the Smaragdine Tablet, 'As above, so below.' Upon earth we see the reflection of the play of the heavenly principles in the actions of men and women. The virgin in her passivity is even as primordial space ere the tides arose. The male is the life-giver. These in the making of life play the active and passive parts. By him she is made creative and fertile; but hers is the child, and he, though the giver of life, passes empty-handed. He spends himself, and nothing remains that is his, save as she calls him mate.

His life is between her hands; his life, that was, and is, and shall be. Therefore should he adore the Passive Principle, for without her he is not. Little knoweth he his need of Her in all the ways of life. She is the Great Goddess.

All the gods are one god, and all the goddesses are one goddess, and there is one initiator.

She is called by many names by many men; but to all she is the Great Goddess, space and earth and water. As space she is called Rhea, mother

of the gods that made the gods; she is more old than time: she is the
matrix of matter; the root-substance of all existence, undifferentiated,
pure. She is also Binah, the Supernal Mother, that receiveth Chokmah, the
Supernal Father. She is the giver of form to the formless force whereby
it can build. She is also the bringer-in of death, for that which has form
must die, outworn, in order that it may be born again to fuller life. All
that is born must die; but that which dies shall be reborn. Therefore
she is called Marah, bitter, Our Lady of Sorrows, for she is the bringer-in
of death. Likewise she is called Ge, for she is the most ancient earth,
the first formed from the formless. All these is she, and they are seen
in her, and whatsoever is of their nature answers unto her, and she hath
dominion over it. Her tides are its tides; her ways are its ways; and whoso
knoweth the one, knoweth the other.

Whatsoever ariseth out of nothingness, she giveth it; whatsoever sinketh
down into nothingness, she receiveth it. She is the Great Sea, whence
life arose, to which all shall return at the end of an aeon.

Herein do we bathe in sleep, sinking back into the primordial deep,
returning to forgotten things before time was: and the soul is renewed,
touching the Great Mother. Whoso cannot return to the primordial, hath
no roots in life, but withereth as the grass. These are the living dead,
they who are orphaned of the Great Mother.

The daughter of the Great Mother is Persephone, Queen of Hades,
ruler of the kingdoms of sleep and death. Under the form of the Dark
Queen men also worship her who is the One: likewise is she Aphrodite.
And herein is a great mystery, for it is decreed that none shall understand
the one without the other.

In death men go to her across the shadowy river, and she is the keeper
of their souls until the dawn. But there is also a death in life, and this
likewise leadeth on to rebirth. Why fear ye the Dark Queen, O men?
She is the Renewer. From sleep we rise refreshed; from death we rise
reborn; by the embraces of Persephone men are made powerful.

For there is a turning-within of the soul whereby men come to
Persephone; they sink back into the womb of time; they become as the
unborn. They enter the kingdom where Persephone rules as Queen;
they are made negative and await the coming of life.

And the Queen of Hades cometh in unto them as a bridegroom, and
they are made fertile for life, and go forth rejoicing for the touch of the
Queen of the kingdoms of sleep hath made them potent.

And even as the Queen of Hades is the daughter of the Great Mother,
so from the Great Sea riseth golden Aphrodite, giver of love. And she

also is Isis after another manner.

She is the Awakener. That which is latent she calleth forth into potency. She is the attraction of outer space, making the centre to manifest. That which is the centre, the all-potent, waiteth, and acheth, unable to brim over and outpour into manifestation until the attraction of outer space draweth upon him.

Equilibrium is fixed in inertia until outer space overset the balance and the All-father pours forth to satisfy the hunger of space. Strange and deep are these truths; verily, they are the keys to the lives of men and women, and unknown to those who worship not the Great Goddess.

Golden Aphrodite cometh not as the virgin, the victim: but as the Awakener, the Desirous One. As outer space she calls, and the All-father commences the courtship. She awakeneth him to desire, and the worlds are created. Lo, She is the Awakener.

That which is potent in the outer is latent in the inner, awaiting the Awakener, unable to brim over until that touch be given; striving in travail as one who cannot bring forth until the Great Goddess changeth the latent into the potent.

How powerful is she, golden Aphrodite the awakener of manhood!

Our Lady is also the Moon, called of some Selene, of others Luna, but by the wise Levanah, for therein is contained the number of Her name. She is the ruler of the tides of flux and reflux. The waters of the Great Sea answer unto her; likewise the waters of all earthly seas, and she ruleth the nature of women.

But there is likewise in the souls of men a flowing and an ebbing of the tides of life, which no one knoweth save the wise. And over these tides the Great Goddess presides under her aspect of the moon. As she passeth from her rising to her setting, so answer these tides unto her. She riseth from the sea as the evening star, and the waters of earth rise in flood. She sinketh as Luna in the western ocean, and the waters flow back into the inner earth and are still in that great lake of darkness wherein are the moon and stars reflected. Whoso is still as the dark underworld lake of Persephone shall see the tides of the Unseen moving therein and shall know all things. Therefore is Luna also called giver of visions.

But all these things are one thing. All these goddesses are one goddess, and we call her Isis, the All-woman, in whose nature all things are found; virgin, and desirous by turn; giver of life and bringer-in of death. She is the cause of creation, for she awakeneth the desire of the All-father and for her sake he createth. Likewise the wise call all women Isis.

She it is who as the Great Sea biddeth him return unto her, sink into her depths, spend himself, and sleep in utter negation. She it is who as Isis of the Underworld awakeneth him with her kisses in the darkness, and he cometh forth by day all-potent as Osiris. She it is who rises from the sea as a star and calleth him to come forth; and he answereth unto her, and the earth grows green with grain. All these things is she, and many more; changing from one to another with the tides of the moon, and the needs of men's souls answer unto her.

In the outer, he is the male, the lord, the giver of life. But in the inner he taketh life at her hands as she bendeth over him, he kneeling. Therefore should he worship the Great Goddess, for without Her he hath no life, and every woman is Her priestess. In the face of every woman let him look for the features of the goddess, watching her phases through the flow and return of the tides to which his soul answereth; awaiting her call, as he needs must, aching in his barrenness.

Each woman is a priestess of the goddess. She is the potent queen of the underworld, whose kisses magnetize and give life. In the inner she is all-potent, she is the fertilizer. She causeth the male to create, for without desire, life goes not forth.

It is her call in the darkness that awakeneth: for in the inner, the male is inert. Not of his own life does he arise, but for desire of her. Until her hands touch him, he is as the dead in the kingdom of the shades; he is death-in-life.

O daughters of Isis, adore the goddess, and in her name give the call that awakens and rejoices. So shall ye be blessed of the goddess and live with fullness of life.

The wise of old beheld all created things as the luminous garment of the Creator: and in the ways of Nature they discerned the ways of God: and they adored God made manifest in Nature, saying, In Nature is God made manifest; therefore let Nature be unto me the manifestation of God.

Isis is the All-woman, and all women are Isis. Osiris is the All-man, and all males are Osiris. Isis is all that is negative, receptive, and latent. Osiris is all that is dynamic and potent. That which is latent in the outer is potent in the inner; and that which is potent in the outer is latent in the inner. Therefore is Isis both Persephone and Aphrodite; and Osiris, the giver of life, is likewise the Lord of the realms of death. This is the law of alternating polarity, which is known to the wise.

Man should not for ever be potent, but should lie latent in the arms of Persephone, surrendering himself. Then she who was dark and cold as outer space before the creative Word, is made queen of the underworld, crowned by his surrender, and her kisses become potent upon his lips.

Awakened by her kisses he shall arise, the all-potent, and his desire shall call golden Aphrodite unto him. But without the kisses of Persephone, he sleepeth in Hades for ever.

And she who is priestess of Isis ruleth over the subtle, inner tides of the hearts of men as Levanah, the moon. As Persephone she draweth him down into the darkness that he may be receptive, negative; as Aphrodite she awakeneth him to light and life. She answereth with her changing phases to the needs of his secret life, and he, fulfilled of her, is made glorious in his strength. And she, so awakening, so calling, so answering, is filled with fullness of life, for she is beloved of the goddess.

6.

Some Helps to Meditation

Meditation may be defined as the practice of concentrated and directed thinking designed to build up an attitude of the mind. It is an exceedingly important part of the discipline that awakens the mind to higher consciousness. Without the regular practice of meditation according to a sound technique, any real achievement is impossible. There are innumerable books upon the subject from many different points of view. Each of these viewpoints has its value, and we shall incline to one or another according to the bias of our characters and the needs of our lives.

Meditation may be considered from four different standpoints. Firstly, that of the development of the personality as such, with a view to a happier and more successful life and the enhancement of the capacities. Secondly, from what may be termed generically the New Thought standpoint, wherein the aim is, broadly speaking, to bring the soul into harmony with God.

Thirdly, from the occult or yoga standpoint. And fourthly, from the mystical standpoint, whether Christian or Non-Christian, wherein the aim is to enable the soul to make the unreserved dedication and unite itself to the Godhead.

It is my belief that the concentration upon any one of these methods to the exclusion of all others, even though this is strenuously recommended by the exponents of the different systems, does not yield the best results in human life-values. It is quite true that the greatest efficiency in the system chosen is gained by such concentration, but the sense of proportion is lost, and the development is one-sided. Consciousness has more than one level, and the development of all the levels in harmonious proportion is needed for the perfection of humanity. None of these systems, left to itself, does this; therefore none of these systems contains the complete curriculum of the perfection of humanity. What shall it profit a man if he gain the whole world and lose his own soul? And is he much better off if he open up the higher aspects of mystical consciousness and lose his physical health? Or achieve the greater power of yoga and sacrifice his mental balance?

I would counsel everyone who takes up the intensive practice of meditation to devise for themselves a discipline which shall include all four aspects, so that the tremendous powers awakened by yoga methods may be disciplined and dedicated by the mystical contacts, and the harmonizing and soothing influence of the New Thought reiterated auto-suggestions may inspire and stabilize the mind, and the commonsense dicta of plain character-building and faculty-development may help to maintain a sense of just proportion.

Meditation is by no means a thing easy of achievement. It is the calisthenics of the soul, and leads on to its acrobatics and athletics. When we first embark upon its practices we shall find that when the first enthusiasm wanes, the mind itself will resist the practices as if with a deliberately willed antagonism. This corresponds to the stiffness of the muscles of an athlete who is out of condition. We all know, however, that the best way to get rid of that painful stiffness is to move the muscles until they warm up and become limber. Such stiffness is best worked off; to try and rest it off is worse than useless. So it is with the mind: we must summon up all our resources of will and perseverance to get through its initial resistance. Once this has been successfully accomplished, and the habit of meditation established, the very resistant inertia of the mind that made the practice of a discipline so difficult will help to maintain it when once the habit has been acquired. We shall be as uneasy and discomforted if we miss our meditation-time as if we miss a meal.

A regular meditation period, with which nothing is allowed to interfere is absolutely essential. A good time is immediately after dressing and before breakfast. The absence of food in the stomach makes meditation much easier, and the activity of dressing ensures that we are sufficiently wide awake not to drift off into dream-land instead of following a train of thought with concentration. For many people, too, the early morning, before the demands of the day take hold upon them, is the only time they can with surety call their own. The mind, fresh from sleep and undistracted is at its best for the contemplation of inner things. There is no better investment we can make towards spiritual or mental progress than this half hour of sacrificed sleep.

It is not a good plan to practise mediation lying in bed before rising, for only a superhuman will can keep us awake under such circumstances, and we shall in all probability deceive ourselves as to the extent to which we are awake, but it is a very good plan to make a habit of turning the thoughts to invocation of the Masters for a few moments immediately on awakening, while consciousness is still on the frontiers of sleep. Such a practice very speedily becomes habitual, and we shall find that we regularly awaken from sleep to find ourselves subconsciously invoking the Masters. Such thought, which often escapes from the limitation of waking consciousness, is very potent.

It is also an excellent plan to go to sleep in contemplation, directing the mind towards some idea or ideal, and allowing the thoughts to circle gently round it until the mind drifts out on the tide of sleep. Concentration should not be attempted. Intruding thoughts should merely be inhibited, and the mind encouraged to brood quietly and almost at random on the chosen idea. After a few nights' practice it will be found that almost before the thoughts are called home and directed to the chosen idea, we have sunk into the most peaceful and refreshing sleep imaginable. And even if sleep does not immediately supervene, and we lie awake for a time, as often occurs with highly-strung people, we are nevertheless resting, for the mind is at peace, and at low tension, and is not thrashing itself to pieces with the bugaboos of anxiety and over-vivid imagination.

There is no better way of going to sleep than in tranquil contemplation of a spiritual ideal, nor is there any surer way of bringing it to birth in our nature.

This should be our routine procedure, night by night, for it is healthful and helpful. It should not be our constant practice to attempt occult feats in sleep, such as telepathy, going up to the Halls of Initiation, or projecting the Astral body. If we do these things too frequently, disturbance of the function of sleep is apt to ensue. These are matters for the trained initiate, who is properly equipped with the necessary Words of Power, symbols, and technique. These things cannot be learnt from books, and should never be attempted except under the proper conditions. And even among initiated adepts it is usual to observe times and seasons in these things, and not to practise them unceasingly.

Another useful practice is that of the Midday Salutation, in which the thoughts are raised to the God of Nature at high noon, the symbol employed being the Sun in Midheaven. This practice soon attunes us to the spiritual essence of nature, and has some very important effects upon consciousness. It is vitalizing and joy-bringing, and harmonizes the whole being, correlating its different aspects, mental, emotional, instinctive, and spiritual, like the notes in a chord.

It is very advantageous, if it can be managed, always to meditate in the same place; but even if we cannot manage always to do our meditation at the identical spot, we can have some symbol which we take out from its covers and set up as the focus of our meditation. We should always have such a meditation symbol. It is the greatest possible help. The student who tries to acquire the habit of meditation without recourse to such extraneous aids is giving himself much unnecessary trouble. Until use is made of such a symbol, its effect will not be believed, moreover, the more it is used, the more potent it grows, for thought-forms are building up around it with every meditation that is performed.

It is essential, for a symbol to develop its full potency, that it should always be kept reverently covered up when not in use, and that we should be extremely discrete as to whom we allow even to look upon it, and no one save the owner should ever lay a finger upon it, and even he should take it in his hands with reverence, saluting it with the appropriate sign, either by crossing himself if the symbol is Christian, or with the sign of his grade if he be an initiate. By these precautions the magnetism which the symbol acquires is prevented from dispersing, and so develops with every meditation performed. For not only is the chosen symbol connected by every law of mental association with the ideal of meditation, but an actual atmosphere is built up around it, and this atmosphere is even more than a thought-form, it is an actual magnetic aura, and its influence is according to its nature.

Its inestimable value lies in its power to recall the wandering thoughts and tune them to the key-note with which it is imbued. The meditations we have performed in its presence during periods of spiritual insight act as mentors during periods of spiritual dryness. It is a storage battery of spiritual force, and like a similar battery on a car, provides the spark that enables the engine to make a start.

The simplest form of symbol for use under unfavourable conditions, such as when travelling, or where privacy is lacking, is a suitable picture or post-card, of some work of art expressive of the aspiration of the soul; or the card may be a plain one of similar size, on which such symbols as are known to the student may be drawn. Little travelling photograph frames of leather or paper cloth, with a piece of talc in place of glass as protection to the picture, and folding flat like a pocket-book, make an excellent little shrine-case. It is a good plan to make an envelope of black silk into which it can be fitted, as this helps to preserve the little shrine from psychic contamination and physical wear and tear.

Where conditions are more favourable, a more elaborate shrine can be constructed, and the most suitable thing for the purpose is a small medicine cupboard that can be fastened to the wall at a convenient height for contemplation. The door of this can be shut when not in use, and when opened out, reveals the interior with its symbolic decoration and objects hallowed by their association with the prayer and aspiration of the soul.

To keep a perpetual light burning before the little shrine costs from three to four shillings a week, because only the purest oil is any use for the purpose; any other kind cakes upon the floating wick and chokes the flame. The proper kind of oil, called sanctuary oil, is sold by any shop that specializes in church furniture or Catholic books and pictures. There too can be obtained the wicks that are used to float on the oil. Any small glass receptacle will do to hold the oil, but these shops also sell the proper sanctuary lamps, which vary from a few pence to beautiful examples of the silversmith's art, costing many pounds. They can be chosen either to stand like a vase, or hang on chains from a bracket-arm. Even if it is not feasible to keep a perpetual light burning before the shrine, it is helpful to have a little lamp to light when meditation is in progress.

Incense also is helpful to the making of an atmosphere which aids concentration. It can be bought either in long joss sticks or cones from any shop that goes in for Oriental goods. A little experimenting will prove which kinds are suitable and which are not. There is an elaborate science of aromatics in relation to states of consciousness, but we cannot enter upon it here. For all practical purposes, any sweet smelling substance, even if it be only smouldering pine cones or lavender stalks, which serves to change the physical atmosphere of a room from that to which we are habituated, will be of assistance in enabling the mind to shift its level from the outer to the inner world.

The ideal incense to use is, of course, that which is sold for use in ritualistic churches, and which is specially compounded of fragrant gums. The drawback to its use for daily meditation is the difficulty of its manipulation, for it has to be burnt upon smouldering charcoal, and the whole affair takes some time to get going, and unless burnt in a swinging censer, goes out capriciously.

There is one thing, however, that can be maintained before even the simplest shrine, or where the tendency of incense to advertise itself all over the house renders its employment inadvisable, and that is the little vase of flowers. There should be something in every shrine that demands daily attention, whether it be the little guarded flame or the little floral offering. There should be some small sacrifice offered daily to keep the spirit of the shrine alive.

A meditation robe is also a great help. It is best formed of thin black silk, or failing that, of some thin cotton stuff, such as mercerized lawn, and should be voluminous enough to swathe the entire figure in ample draperies, including long loose sleeves to fall over the hands and a monk's cowl to pull over the head. When not in use it should go into a black silk case and be put away apart from the ordinary clothes. The whole idea underlying the material precautions taken to protect sacred things from profanation or demagnetization, which is the same thing, is based upon the analogy of electricity. The subtle force which is woven into intangible forms by the power of the mind, and which is the link between mind and matter, is electromagnetic in nature, and if we work by electrical analogies when dealing with its subtle manifestations, we shall not go far wrong. The most effective material for insulation is black silk.

All this paraphernalia may seem strange to any one accustomed to the simplicities of Protestant prayer, but if experimented with, its efficacy will soon be realized. We are not under any delusion that it has any effect upon the disposition of God, to incline Him favourably towards the user, nor upon spiritual forces, to cause them to flow in fanciful channels, but it has a very marked effect upon the consciousness of those who employ it, and it is for this reason that we recommend its use to those commencing upon the practice of meditation. The experienced meditator may be independent of all such devices, but the beginner in what is actually an art of no small difficulty, will find them of great assistance.

7.

Teachings Concerning the Aura

The aura is a less simple structure than is often supposed. It may be conceived of as an ovoid sphere extending to arm's length beyond the physical body. The aura's size and clarity vary according to its owner's development.

The ovoid sphere usually consists of a magnetic field containing three concentric levels or layers which in fact interpenetrate each other but which are clairvoyantly perceived as bands of different colours. Permeating and conditioning this magnetic field is a dual circuit of Force—the Cosmic Current of the microcosm—which develops throughout evolution and which links the Divine Spark to the magnetic core of the earth during each incarnation.

The central circuit of this Current gives the human being his energy and the peripheral circuit (which arises out of the central) is concerned with the organization of that energy. In the central circuit also is that part of the aura which is in contact with the Great Unmanifest.

As seen by clairvoyance the vehicles of the human being emanate bands of auric force which appear as coloured strata of different types. The aura is not necessarily observed by clairvoyance each time in its entirety. Sometimes only one band is seen at a time and the rest is either dim or invisible. The three bands, when the aura is seen in its entirety, may be described as follows.

I. *The magnetic or health aura.* This is the innermost band of the auric field, since it is clairvoyantly seen to emanate from the physical body and its condition indicates that body's health. This emanation varies from a faint greyish cloud to a strong silvery light. It has been sometimes asserted that the aura is electric and if this is true there may be means found for detecting it since scientific instruments already exist such as the electro-cardiagraph and the electro-encephalograph for discovering the body's electricity. Long ago a claim was made by Kilner that the aura could be thus registered but prejudice and over-statement disqualified

TEACHINGS CONCERNING THE AURA   141

the pretensions of the Kilner Screens.

II.   Next to the health aura, clairvoyance perceives an area suffused with colours denoting the predominating mood or temperament. This is the astral aura. In this section there will be a preponderance of yellow if the person be intellectual or of blue if he be musical. Art, materialism, love, lust, fear and depression are equally observed in their corresponding tints in these astral emanations.

'Chakras', 'Lotuses' or 'Wheels' of force are really in all levels of the aura but those popularized in text-books usually refer to the astral section and are at seven important points therein which correlate with the nervous sytem.

III.   The outermost band of auric substance stretching out beyond the astral links up with the Individuality. This band seen clairvoyantly, is composed of rainbow colours and of rays of light. It holds contacts with the Essential Self, non-human beings and other Cosmic Potencies as well as with Esoteric Guides of past and present lives. It is here also that indications of spiritual connection with esoteric groups can be discerned.

These three 'sections' of the aura represent the etheric, astro-mental and spiritual levels of consciousness which are 'seen' to be developed or otherwise according to the brilliancy and size of the bands of light portraying them clairvoyantly. Auras of Masters can extend to a much greater degree than those of less evolved men and if a Master is working in conjunction with his pupil, the latter's aura is often enclosed within the Master's as well as being itself much expanded.

An exercise said to be useful to help in seeing the aura is to focus the eyes on space, gazing through the person being studied. then imagine him as a nude astral figure round which the three bands of the aura spontaneously build up.

For such work you will use the pineal gland or centre of awareness between the eyebrows. As is well known, all psychic experiments must be kept under control of the will and must not be tried when tired or emotionally disturbed. It should also be unnecessary to emphasize here that such visions only take place subjectively. It will be found that when the third band of the aura (linking with the Higher Self) is being inspected, consciousness will be spiritually exalted and tend to diffusion into the Higher Self; whereas when the astral and etheric bands of the aura are being studied, personal consciousness will be magically concentrated on those planes.

The Tree of Life should be built up in the aura and much realization as to character and development can be experienced by the manner in which the Sephiroth and Pillars appear. It is also helpful to build up in the same way the astrological chart and observe the influences which this chart may suggest. It is, however, well to bear in mind that astrology should be treated neither as 'an exact science' nor as a superstition, but as an illuminative method of analysis and philosophy.

There are various books on the aura which will repay study. Specially recommended are those by C. W. Leadbeater and his pupil A. E. Powell. Further teaching on this subject of auras by Dion Fortune is here appended. This concerns the aura in relation to Polarity.

The central circuit of magnetic force in the aura, passing between the Divine Spark and the soul of the earth, is the basic factor of individual manifestation. It may be conceived of as emanating from the Divine Spark, looping round the magnetic core of the earth, and returning to the Divine Spark again. It is the passing of the current through the magnetic core of the earth that determines incarnation. The secondary magnetic circuit in the aura, the Peripheral Circuit, arises out of the emanations of the primary circuits, interacting with environmental factors. This circuit is sensitive to the changing play of these factors; whereas the primary, central circuit is immune to all external influences. Between the two is a magnetic field, the aura itself. Within the aura are different forms of activity, and these give rise to the multicoloured bands described by clairvoyants.

The central circuit remains unaffected by all extraneous conditions, its voltage rising and falling, and the direction of the flow of the current changing according to esoteric constant factors. The peripheral circuit, however, is highly sensitive, the centres in it corresponding to the external factors reacting to every change in these factors—such changes being due to the permutations and combinations of the cosmic factors, reinforcing, modifying or counteracting each other as is described in the judging of a horoscope.

The available energy in an aura is derived from its central magnetic circuit, but the organization of that energy within the aura is affected by the influences to which the peripheral circuit is exposed. These set up currents within the magnetic field of the two circuits. These cross-currents establish equilibrium in the course of time, and become stabilized centres and systems, as described in the *Cosmic Doctrine*. Although that teaching refers actually to the genesis of the universe, it is equally applicable to the development of the aura of the individual. The Tree of Life is a cross-section of the aura. What is true of it is also true of the universe.

The more highly developed the aura, the greater what may best be described as its surface tension—a kind of skin of resistance formed by the interweaving of magnetic circuits. These arise from outgoing rays of emanation obeying the law of the curvature of force and returning upon themselves at their point of emanation. The tension gradually increases, causing, as it were, a shrinking and tightening of the circuits, until finally a tensely resistive surface of magnetic loops is established. This constitutes the exterior envelope of the aura.

This phase having been reached, the tension within the magnetic field rises steadily because force is no longer being lost, the Rays being re-entrant. Now comes the time when openings can be made in the aura and rays of force projected, for sufficient force has now been accumulated for such projections to be possible. But be it observed that these emanations are from the magnetic field and not from the central circuit. This fact explains certain discrepancies that may have appeared in the teaching. All exchange of magnetism takes place from the field of induction, not from the central circuit, which is the source of the energy. The primal source of all force, the Divine Spark in the Great Unmanifest, possesses infinite energy, and is therefore unaffected by such emanations or losses, but the potential of the magnetic field is affected by them, just as it is changed in its modes and distribution by the influences affecting the peripheral circuit.

The more highly evolved the surface organization of the aura, however, the less it is affected by external influences, save where centres for the reception of different types of force are developed. In the course of the evolution of an aura, then, it goes through the following phases: a primary phase of complete unresponsiveness to all influences save the flux and reflux of the central magnetic current, which corresponds to the pre-natal life of the Personality or Lower Self; a developing phase during which sensitivity is increasing, which corresponds to the youth of the incarnated Personality; a mature phase during which the receptivity of the periphery is being brought into equilibrium with the resistiveness of the central core and thus under the control of the Divine Spark; and a final phase during which receptivity is lessening and the activity of the now highly developed aura is concentrating around the fluctuations of the central circuit.

These phases take place in the course of an evolution. Each incarnation sees the resumption of the different forms of activity which characterize the different planes of manifestation; each discarnation sees the discontinuance of such forms of activity, but the activity of the central core never ceases during the whole course of evolution, and it is its perpetual flux, reflux and permutations which constitute the ever-changing pattern of existence. All things are reducible to these terms and when thus reduced become explicable and predictable. By an understanding of the nature and interplay of these factors, the control of the forces manifesting within the auric sphere can be attained. The Personality, which builds up out of the emanations of the peripheral circuit, is negative to its environment and conditioned thereby; but the Individuality or Higher Self is organized around the central magnetic core, and is responsive to the influence of the Divine Spark, which obeys laws that are beyond our comprehension as incarnate beings, and are comprehensible only in terms of the consciousness that can rise to the plane where they operate. This knowledge, however, can be translated and transmitted by reflection and deduction in consciousness suitably conditioned, and it is the work of the Mysteries to effect such conditioning, and also to teach the Lore of the Peripheral Circuit in its relationship to the universe.

Upon this theoretical basis all practical occult tradition is built up, and it should be thoroughly grasped by those who would make of the occult arts a science. The practical teaching is based upon, and explicable by, the principles outlined in these teachings upon the aura. It must always be borne in mind that the aura is fundamentally a self-contained unit unaffected by external conditions; that it starts its evolution in this state, and returns to it, after passing through a phase of susceptibility to modifications in its activities by external influences, but immune from any alteration in its basic organization and existence. After a certain point in its development is reached, it becomes increasingly independent of external influences, but up to that point, though not dependent upon such influences for its existence, it is dependent upon them for the stimulation of its activities, and can equally be subject to the inhibiting or deforming of its development through their unbalanced or adverse influence—adverse, that is to say, to a given phase of activity.

Once a state of independence of external influence has been reached by the development in centres within the aura corresponding to the external factors—centres that can specialize the activities of the primary energy of the central circuit in the same way as the cosmic centres so specialize it—the entity can, by closing all outgoing emanations, raise the voltage of its magnetic field and so have energy available for the projection of emanations. It can determine the type of these emanations, as distinguished from a general radiation of energy, if it is able to close its sphere to all external influences and generate energy of a specific type by the concentration of the basic energy in a given centre. This is the method of the adepti.

When complete immunity from external influences is achieved, the entity is completely self-acting. During the intermediate phases of acquiring sensitivity and achieving the control of, and determining immunity to sensitivity, the skilful use of stimuli is a valuable technique of function; likewise the skilful use of the art of immunization which is its corollary. Sensitivity to stimuli is achieved by concentration on the peripheral circuit; immunization by the concentration on the central circuit. To achieve these techniques, the imagination visualizes the circuits as diagrammatic glyphs with the aid of the Tree of Life and that simplified chart of the heavens which is used for astrological purposes. The Tree of Life is used in relation to the central circuit; and the chart of the heavens in relation to the peripheral circuit. The adept builds these up as clearly visualized pictures, the former of his aura, and the latter of his environment. For simplicity's sake they are highly stylized pictures, symbolic, and charged with mythical meaning. The story of Guinevere is such a myth related to the Glyph of Yesod, Hod, and Netzach. The myths relate to the force aspect and the glyphs to the form aspect of manifestation.

8.

Pitfalls of Spiritual Healing

The question of healing has always been of prime interest to students of occultism. Discovering the great increase of our knowledge that comes through the doctrines of esoteric science, they cannot fail to realize that it has a practical application in the field of therapeutics. The idealist is especially drawn towards mystical and transcendental studies, and his strong compassionate impulse leads him to desire above all things to lift the burden of suffering from the world. He is acutely conscious of the limitations of the orthodox methods and keenly anxious for a way of escape from those limitations. The humanitarian impulse and the zeal of the discoverer have between them made of the occult field a prolific breeding-ground for all manner of new ideas in therapeutics and hygiene.

The Fraternity I work with, being a society for the study of esotericism in all its branches, is frequently asked whether it has any healing circles among its students, or any classes wherein spiritual healing is taught; and when it replies that it has none of these things,[1] it is asked whether it condemns spiritual healing and advises its students against its practice. It may be well, therefore, to define its position lest misunderstanding arise upon the one side or the other.

It is not possible in this matter to give an unqualified yes or no. It is necessary to clear the ground and classify the subject-matter before we can do justice to it. But we may briefly indicate our attitude by saying that we believe in spiritual healing but disbelieve in spiritual healers. Does this mean that we are not interested in spiritual healing? No, it does not. Being a Fraternity of the Tradition which recognizes Aesculapius and Paracelsus, we can hardly reckon the question of therapeutics as alien to us. It means that we take the matter so seriously that we are disinclined to play with it, or suffer it to be played with if it is within

---

[1] At the time of writing. Ed.

our power to prevent it. While we are fully alive to the possibilities of spiritual healing, we cannot shut our eyes to the unsatisfactory and even disastrous results that ensue when it is ignorantly or inadequately employed. We desire to see spiritual healing done, but we want to see it done in the right way and under the right conditions so that the patient shall have the best possible chance that can be afforded him, and that chance is not afforded him when the person who takes charge of his case is ignorant of the problems presented by his condition.

Good intentions are no substitute for sound knowledge. Just as the materialists are wrong when they hold man to consist of his physical body and nothing else, so are the mystics wrong when they act as if man were a spirit and nothing else. Man is a sevenfold being, and it is not possible to separate one aspect of his nature from another for any practical purpose, for they are interacting.

The only satisfactory healer is the one who has an adequate knowledge of the fourfold nature of man, can diagnose in terms of each of the aspects of manifesting life and treat each level of manifestation according to its needs. Each plane of manifestation has its own laws and conditions; the spiritual plane is governed by spiritual law; the mental plane by the laws of the functioning of mind; the astral plane has its own laws, and so have the etheric sub-planes of matter; dense matter itself is also a kingdom which has a constitutional government.

This does not mean, however, that each plane is autonomous. Each level is ruled and ensouled by the next subtlest level, the physical by the etheric, the etheric by the astral, the astral by the mental, and the mental by the spiritual. But although the subtler levels rule and ensoul each its denser neighbour, they rule as constitutional monarchs according to the laws of the country, and not as arbitrary autocrats. Mind can influence matter profoundly, and yet it cannot do just as it pleases with matter. It must always rule by availing itself of the inexorable laws of the physical plane. Even the most extreme school of spiritual healing does not expect a man to grow a new limb; it is content if the repair processes take place naturally by the gradual and normal reconstruction of tissue. In fact, it is content to focus the *vis medicatrix naturae* at the required spot and let the healing take place by natural means.

The great mistake which the spiritual healers make is to refuse to recognize the fact that each plane has its own laws, and that these laws are both the means and the limitations of their art. The great mistake which the materialistic school of medicine makes is to refuse to recognize the fact that each level of manifestation is operated and directed from a subtler plane and that the happenings and reactions of that subtler plane have got to be reckoned with. The practitioner of orthodox medicine is the heir of generations of systematized research into the nature of the physical machine and has a pretty comprehensive understanding of it. He knows what to do if the systems of levers and pulleys we call our limbs come off their rollers; in other words, he can reduce a dislocation. if the length of piping which is the human intestine gets a kink in it, he knows the only thing to do is to open up the casing of the machine and disentangle it. If this is not done, the soul withdraws from its useless instrument because no amount of spiritual force is going to drive material substance through a kinked tube, as many a spiritual healer has learnt to his cost. The mundane practitioner, in fact, thoroughly understands the mechanics of the body.

Concerning its chemistry he has a certain amount of understanding, but his knowledge is by no means so complete. He can reproduce in a test-tube the processes of digestion; he can mix chemical ingredients and produce an artificial digestive juice which is just as good as the natural one. But here he is trenching upon the life-processes, and he does not understand the nature of life. He cannot tell why it is that under the influence of painful emotion, such as fear, hate or grief, the stomach will change the nature of the digestive juices it secretes so that they become useless or even actually poisonous. He may be able to reproduce in his test-tube the secretions, but he cannot reproduce the influences of emotion upon those secretions.

The spiritual healer, on the other hand, can influence the emotions, calm, transmute, and direct them. He and he alone can cure the dyspepsia which comes from a chronic perversion of the digestive juices by chronic emotional distress.

But just as that hydra-headed complaint called stomach-ache may have its origin in a disturbance of the subtle, emotional aspect of man which acts as the regulator of metabolism, so it may have its origin in a disturbance of the mechanics or hydraulics of digestion. The one case calls for spiritual methods, the other for surgical methods, and that quickly. Who is to decide which it is to be? The only person who is competent to make a diagnosis is the man who has been trained in a general hospital and has seen every variety of disease in the living and the dead; the man who has a clear-cut mental picture of the hidden machinery of the body and the appearances, gross and microscopical, of the processes of disease. He alone knows what is happening and can form a just estimate, for he alone can read the significance of the physical signs.

It is for this reason that, although as occultists we have a theory of disease and of therapy, we are diffident concerning the practice of spiritual healing. It is not because we dispute the validity of spiritual healing when applied to a suitable case, but because we distrust the power of diagnosis of the spiritual healer and recognize his liability to get hold of an unsuitable case and make a most lamentable mess of it. It is all very well for the fanatical adherent of spiritual healing to say that God is omnipotent and that spirit is all and matter nothing; I am not prepared to argue the metaphysics of the case; the final court of appeal must always be experience, and experience, unfortunately, does not bear out their contention. Spiritual healing has its limits, whether spiritual healers admit it or not. They are far from being uniformly successful, as they would be if their hypothesis were correct.

Because God is omnipotent does not mean that He is as arbitrary and incalculable as an Eastern despot. May we not conceive that He works through law, and that His omnipotence lies in the inviolable nature of His laws? Are not the laws and limitations of matter just as much His ordinances as the laws of spirit? When a so-called spiritual healing results in the cure of bodily ills, it has, *ipso facto*, become a physical healing. A spiritual healing that remained literally a spiritual healing would never take effect on the plane of matter at all. Spiritual force must be transmuted down the planes and manifest in matter in order that a change of physical condition may take place.

Equally, may it not be that the successful result of medical treatment or of an operation should really be accounted a spiritual healing? If it is our karma to die, we die, despite anything that can be done for us; if it is our karma to recover, why should not the spiritual forces manifest through the skill of the surgeon as well as through the mind of the healer? Why do we rope off any section of the healing art and say that here God does not operate? All healing is spiritual, when rightly understood, because life itself, in essence, is spirit.

It is this unhappy antagonism between the materialist and mystic exponents of the healing art that is to be deplored. The patient needs both, for it is not possible for any level of the composite man to be afflicted without the disturbance spreading up and down the planes, and repair is never a process of one plane only.

In judging the suitability of a case for spiritual healing there is another factor to be considered as well as the physical nature of the complaint, and that is the spiritual status of the patient. Is it justifiable to use spiritual forces to restore a physical sense of well-being to a materially-minded man suffering from over-indulgence? Is it justifiable to accept as a subject for spiritual healing a person who cares nothing whatever for spiritual things and merely wants to be relieved of his discomfort?

Before we can answer this question we must answer another. What is a spiritual healing? For there are several kinds of non-physical healing, and not all of them are spiritual.

True spiritual healing is really character-healing whereby karma is ab-reacted and the patient freed from the after-effects of forces he himself has set going in the past. By far the greater part of what is loosely called spiritual healing is really mental healing wherein the power of the mind over the body is exploited, and it has no more real claim to be called spiritual than has Coué's method of auto-suggestion to which it is closely akin. Baudouin, making his marvellous analysis of Coué's method in his most valuable book, *Suggestion and Auto-suggestion* reveals the *modus operandi* of all non-physical healing, showing exactly how the subconscious mind manipulates the body. It is always emotion, not will, which is the driving force. In the case of a spiritual healing, it is a spiritual emotion derived from mystical experience. In the case of mental healing by suggestion, which is what the greater proportion of non-physical healing really is, it is the emotion of faith and hope induced by the prestige of the healer which is the motive power of the change of consciousness that effects the healing.

When the healer is alleged to be a discarnate spirit, this contention is not invalidated, for surely if we have learnt anything from occult science, we have learnt that death makes no difference to us, we have only shed our bodies. The spirit healer merely has to his advantage the added prestige of being something unusual.

Though the force that heals may be purely spiritual in its inception, it nevertheless has to be translated down the planes before it can take effect on this physical body. Mind cannot manipulate matter, but mind can manipulate the etheric double which is the matrix of matter. But as Baudouin has shown, the level of the mind which is in touch with the etheric double is beyond the reach of the will. We must therefore, in seeking to manipulate it, find a substitute for the directing influence of the conscious will; we find this in the spontaneous effect of emotion working through an image in the imagination.

Genuine emotion—and none other has adequate motive power— cannot be produced at will. Coué realized this, and found his substitute for emotion in long-continued attention, hence his introduction of the knotted piece of string and the repetition of a formula. In true spiritual healing the alterative emotion is evoked by mystical experience. In the average mental healing it is evoked by the prestige of the practitioner. In psychic healing it is produced by telepathic suggestion. In all cases the *modus operandi* is the same, the automatic mind of the patient, the lowest level of subconsciousness which controls the etheric double, is manipulated and is the vehicle of the healing.

As soon as we touch the subconscious mind we touch the hidden springs of the personality, and whoever does this exceedingly potent thing needs to know what he is about. Nothing is more misleading than the obvious in this sphere. The subconscious mind, when disturbed, turns itself upside down, transfers its emotions from their real object to a symbol, and tangles the trail beyond all disentangling by anyone but an expert psychologist. Nowhere are fools more ready to rush in than in the sphere of comforting emotional disturbance. Someone tells them a pathetic and plausible tale and they accept it unquestioningly. Little do they realize what is at work below the surface.

Take the following case as an example; it is typical of many. A man possessing a good deal of personality and magnetism finds that he is able to help people, to cheer them when depressed, to vitalize them when weary, and even relieve pain by his touch, and he sets up as a spiritual healer. He may or may not, in addition to these primary qualifications, study naturotherapy or manipulative treatment; his chief stock-in-trade, however, is his personal influence. He has what is called in the orthodox healing profession, a good bedside manner. He is probably able to help a great many people in various ways, his chief asset being that he gets them to help themselves in a way that the medical practitioner who relies solely on his pharmacopoeia, is unable to do. He probably has in him the makings of a first-class doctor, but the opportunity to qualify has been denied him. His natural intuitiveness and shrewdness are soon reinforced by practical experience, and he probably reads medical books as well and acquires a smattering of ideas on the subject. All goes well for a time, he does some good and no lasting harm, as the naturopathic remedies are not drastic. One can play a great many coloured lights on people without doing them any damage and put them on to some very queer diets without giving them anything worse than the hiccoughs. Mental and spiritual methods of treatment in normal people, are at worst ineffectual, and do not produce drastic reactions.

There are, however, certain pitfalls in his path which he is not in a position to avoid, as will be clearly seen when they are explained. Among his patients are certain cases complaining of exactly the same symptoms;

they are easily tired, depressed, out of sorts, and with feelings of ill-defined malaise; not really ill, yet never well, with, perhaps, various odd symptoms thrown in as make-weights. Anyway, whatever may be the matter with them, the human machine is running badly. He applies approximately the same treatment to all of them, treatment which has benefited many other cases with similar symptoms. Now let us consider their history, and let me say that these cases are not imaginary; I have seen many of each type.

Case No. 1 reacts to the treatment by exploding like a bomb. It is a case of sex repression and the dammed-up forces are let loose upon the unfortunate healer, his magnetism having proved all too effective; and as hell knows no fury like a woman scorned, she tells all her friends that he has attempted to outrage her, and they probably believe her, for a more fiercely virginal person could not possibly be imagined; she may ultimately go to the police with her tale, but here she will get a less sympathetic reception, for it is an old story here, and the police are wise in human nature.

Now what would the qualified medical man do with such a case? He does not put much faith in symptoms that are unaccompanied by signs. He knows that if the patient complains of feeling unusual sensations there will be something to show for it somewhere; it may be in the blood seen under the microscope; it may be in an electro-cardiograph of the heart; one or another of the innumerable modern methods of diagnosis will reveal something abnormal somewhere. The qualified man has at his disposal resources which are denied to his unorthodox rival, and with their aid he is able to explain the abnormality in terms of physiological function, which is the only real solution of any problem of disease. He quickly detects the hysterical case because he knows that the symptoms she complains of ought to be accompanied by corresponding signs. When these are lacking he does not attempt to treat the physical condition, which is probably not in need of treatment, but sends his patient for psychological treatment and the specialist who deals with the case never sees her alone because he knows what is at the bottom of her trouble.

Surely it is obvious, when one understands the mechanism of such a case, that to pour more life-force into a person who is already suffering from congested life-force is to provoke a catastrophe?

Now let us consider case No. 2. The symptoms are much the same. Treatment is given, and an improvement, possibly considerable improvement, results. The patient is able to take up activities that have had to be given up. The case is hailed as a cure. The healer's reputation and self-confidence go up. Presently, however, the case begins to go downhill again gradually; treatment is renewed; improvement results. Cured again. Then once more the trouble starts. Treated again, cured again. Does it occur to anybody to notice that the exacerbations take place at the rise of the sap and the fall of the leaf and ease off when the change of season is established?

Then one day something occurs which cannot be ignored: the patient suddenly collapses with blood pouring from the mouth to the horror of everyone, and the healer most of all. Most people know what that means. A doctor is called in and says, 'If I had seen this case when the trouble first showed itself, it could have been cured; now it is only a matter of time till the end.'

But that is not all. The doctor will want to examine what he calls 'contacts', the people who have been in close touch with the patient, and when he does so he will find some of the adults and most of the children have been infected, for tuberculosis is infectious and children are especially susceptible.

And now for case No. 3. We have much the same tale, vague ill-health and some slight local symptoms. It does not yield to spiritual treatment, but the treatment is persevered with. A home-made diagnosis is arrived at and various nature-cure remedies are tried, without result. When the case finally comes into medical hands the diagnosis is cancer too far gone for operation.

Finally, let us consider the lesson case No. 4 has to teach us. The same history as before. Nothing much to show for it, but chronic ill-health. Then things become worse, the symptoms declare themselves obviously as paralysis, heart trouble, kidney trouble, anything. The spiritual healer recognizes the nature of the complaint all right, it stares him in the face. And what is the ultimate diagnosis in this case? The doctor is not quite so ready with it as the spiritual healer, though he does not deny his interpretation of the symptoms; the heart or the kidneys are involved right enough, that is agreed. Nevertheless, he takes a specimen of the patient's blood for examination. Presently he prescribes a course of treatment which will last two years. The case clears up rapidly, and yet the doctor will not let his patient go, but insists that the treatment continue. He also says there must be no more children till the end of the two years, and when we see what the child is like who is born before the treatment commenced, we are not surprised. Why is it that the doctor can cure this patient and God cannot? Perhaps God does not particularly want to under the circumstances. When Our Lord healed one of the sufferers who came to Him, he said, 'Go, and sin no more.' But I do not suppose it ever occurred to the spiritual healer to say this to his patient, nor did he think to ask questions concerning a long-forgotten moral lapse.

There are three diseases which between them are responsible for more ill health than all the others put together; they are all three insidious in their onset, multiform in their symptoms, striking any structure in the body and producing different effects in different cases; they are all amenable to treatment at the outset and incurable when well established; and they all three need to be diagnosed by means of laboratory tests, and two of the three can be given to other people by the sufferer. Is the spiritual healer in a position to recognize the incipient stages of tuberculosis, cancer and syphilis? I have spent all my life in circles that went in for unorthodox healing of one kind or another, and I have seen so many of the resistant cases which turned out in the end to be one or another of these three that although I am not prepared to say that spiritual forces cannot heal them, I think we are justified in concluding that they are extremely resistant to spiritual healing and that far better results are obtained by physical methods if they are applied in the early stages. But in saying these hard things of spiritual healing, I do not wish to discredit it *en bloc*.

I have seen cases of serious illness in which the diagnosis was as well established as it was possible to be, healed by spiritual means when all physical resources had failed; and I have seen cases that were healings right enough in that the patient was cured of hysteria, though these were not the cures of dire physical maladies that they were reputed to be; but these two types of cure form but a small percentage of a most deplorable morass of sheer foolishness, credulity and charlatanry.

The weakness of spiritual healing lies in two things; firstly in the inability of the spiritual healer, whatever may be his healing powers, to make a diagnosis and determine what cases are suitable for his ministrations and what are not; and while he is trying his methods and finding out, the time may have gone by when a cure was possible in the case of the three dread scourges referred to. Relying on the power of God, the spiritual healer, at the beginning of his career, will take on anybody who has still got the breath of life in them. In fact I have myself seen several cases of attempts to raise the dead. Later in his career, however, he is usually more cautious unless he is a charlatan, and then he diagnoses, not his patient's disease, but his credulity and his purse. It is this refusal of the spiritual healer to recognize his limitations which does so much harm, for spiritual healing can be very valuable when used in its proper sphere.

Secondly, although there are practitioners of spiritual healing who obtain results in suitable cases, it is my experience that the general run of people who come to me and tell me that they want to take up spiritual healing have got two things in common, a complete innocence of any scientific knowledge and an equally complete ignorance of life's problems. They rush in where angels fear to tread, and in all too many cases the poet's classification of them is correct. They are either well-meaning and rash, or mercenary charlatans. The few, the very few, who fall into neither of these classifications, are not among those who advertise their wares in the many trashy little periodicals that cater for the spiritual equivalent of the get-rich-quick and gold brick industries.

I do not think it is possible for a spiritual healer to make a profession of his powers, taking all comers like a panel doctor. Real spiritual healing is a thing that goes very deep and there are very few cases to which it can rightly be applied, and the choice of these cases does not depend upon the nature of the disease but upon the spiritual condition of the patient.

It is to my mind a lamentable thing that spiritual healing should ever have been allowed to become separated from physical healing, for every sick man needs both, though the proportions in which he needs them vary in different cases. The ideal doctor is one who, like the ancients, is priest as well as physician; but such are rare, and what shall we do to cope with our immediate problems that are pressing for solution? To whom shall we entrust our case in the unhappy state of affairs prevailing among us, in which we have to choose between a doctor who knows nothing about our souls and a spiritual healer who knows nothing about our bodies? The choice is often a difficult one, and it is greatly to be regretted that spiritual and physical healing should thus be divorced, for a patient has both mind and body.

Personally I do not think they should be, nor need they be if neither party were fanatical and each limited himself to his own province. Spiritual healing is, after all, of the kingdom of the spirit, and no doctor interferes with his patient's religious convictions; the spiritual healer, unfortunately, seems to think that although, according to his hypothesis, material remedies have no power to cure disease, they have plenty of power to interfere with his treatment and prevent it from being effectual. Nor has he any scruples about passing from the plane where he has knowledge to the plane where he has no adequate experience, and directing the physical régime.

It appears to me that our wisest course, until such time as the ideal shall be available, is to entrust our sick bodies to the man who has the widest experience and the best equipment, that is to say, the qualified medical man, and to supplement his efforts with the ministrations of a spiritual healer if we feel we need them. No reasonable doctor would object to what are, strictly speaking, the ministrations of religion, provided that the spiritual healer restricts his efforts to spiritual matters and leaves the physical plane alone, as he would be well advised to do. If his efforts are successful, the doctor will report the success. When all is said and done, the main thing is that a suffering body should be eased and a suffering soul tranquillized; not the manner in which credit is to be apportioned between rival practitioners and their methods.

Approached in this way, a rapprochement is possible; but no doctor is going to tolerate the interference of a spiritual healer who pulls against him and advises the discarding of his remedies and the disregarding of his advice. The patient will abandon his remedies quickly enough, and with the doctor's consent, when the cure has been effected. It is fanaticism on the one hand, and a not unjustifiable exasperation on the other, which makes the difficulties.

No doubt many of the prejudices we deplore originated in the phases through which medicine went in the course of its history. In mediaeval times, when the Church dominated every detail of society, all healing was spiritual in that its appeal was almost exclusively to faith and imagination and was combined with the most complete disregard of common sense. Ambrose Paré, the father of surgery, might well say, 'I dressed his wounds and God healed him', in other words, 'I let him alone and gave nature a chance'.

When the medical mind shook off not only the dominance of the Church but also the prestige of the ancients and relied exclusively on experiment and observation, progress was extraordinarily rapid, and results so fruitful that the spiritual factor was completely overwhelmed and vanished from the medical purview. The only person who remembered it was the patient, and his voice got little hearing in the age of reason which saw the development of modern medicine.

With the coming of the New Psychology, however, the mental factor in the human make-up has been forced upon the attention of the medical world and is receiving more and more recognition. It is difficult to pick up the current number of any medical journal and not find, somewhere in its pages, a reference to this factor, and those who give it most weight are among the most prominent men in their profession.

So far, so good, and such recognition of a non-physical factor in physiology is a great gain, but it does not go far enough, as its exponents will soon discover. There is a spiritual as well as a mental factor to be reckoned with in dealing with human beings, and the weakness of psychology lies in the fact that it has no means of measuring or dealing with this factor. Psychoanalysis may take a mind to pieces expertly enough, but it does not very frequently succeed in putting it together again and making it work. To my way of thinking, it is a method of diagnosis rather than of treatment. The only person who ever succeeds in putting a mind together again is the spiritual healer in the true sense of the word, because he alone possesses any knowledge of the only synthetic principle in the nature of man, and that is the spiritual principle around which all the rest is built up, the Divine Spark which is the nucleus of his being.

When the mind is taken to pieces, it is this vital nucleus, the basis of each individualized existence, which is laid bare; and when the mind is put together again it must be reconstructed in relation to this nucleus. When we remember, moreover, that this nucleus does not exist by and of itself, but is of the nature of a ray from the Central Sun of Life, we shall see that no reconstruction can be adequate which takes no account of its relation to its source.

And equally, if man is a fourfold being of body, emotions, mind and spirit, he must dwell in a fourfold environment, of physical, astral, archetypal and spiritual conditions. These must all be understood and taken account of by whosoever would heal the whole man. But where are we to find such physicians as these?

Esoteric science alone holds the key to the situation because the initiate alone has an understanding of the planes of existence and is equipped to cope with them. It is too much to hope that the day will ever come when the medical profession as a whole will be a temple of initiates; the gifts that make the initiated priest-physician are rare, and there is a vast amount of honest spade-work which must be done by less gifted men. But I hope and believe that the day will come when human thought as a whole, and not only that of the medical schools, will recognize the part played by the emotions and imagination in our physical states in both health and disease; when everyone will have some elementary knowledge of the hygiene of right thinking just as school children are taught simple ideas concerning the hygiene of the physical body; and that we shall all recognize that we can poison each other with harmful suggestions, even if kindly meant.

Every medical student ought to be taught the power of the mind over the body and trained to utilize it in his work; every probationer in a hospital ought to be drilled in the psychology of suggestion as she is drilled in the technique of asepsis till it becomes second nature, and she would no more think of ignoring the part played by the imagination and emotional states in the welfare of a patient than she would think of taking unsterilized instruments from one bed to another.

This is the most we can hope for within the realm of practical politics, and it is my belief that this state of things is nearer than might be believed and that the present generation will see its establishment, among the heads of the profession at any rate.

Science is, after all, not a body of arcana, but a method of dealing with any sort of facts, from market-gardening to metaphysics. The essence of science does not lie in knowledge, but in method. It is here that the quack differs from the trained man; he may have acquired a liberal proportion of the trained man's knowledge, but he lacks his method and the disciplined mind which is the basis of his method. Consequently his knowledge will always be a rule-of-thumb affair, having no basic principle.

Speaking for myself, I have little faith in the untrained mind, and little love for the impractical dreamer, however idealistic. I have therefore never attempted to put into practice the knowledge of esoteric medicine which has come down to me as part of the heritage of the Western esoteric tradition; neither have I been willing to impart it to the many spiritual and psychic healers who at one time or another have got into touch with us and asked for this information, for I have seen too much harm result from their untutored efforts to have any faith left in them. The only people who can rightly use this knowledge are the men and women who have already got the necessary basis of scientific training and clinical experience. The therapy of the subtle body must be grafted on to the rootstock of the therapy of the dense body because for all practical purposes they cannot be separated until death parts them permanently.

9.

Power Tides and Cycles

The very word 'tide' implies a rise and fall in time, and in considering the power tides we should have in mind the idea of rise and fall, no matter how vast or how small may be that tide. We are also taught that with regard to evolution 'all is cyclic', and that, in addition to the great cycles of time coming round on their orbits, they also tend to rise as consciousness develops, so we are bidden to 'think spirally'.

The Cosmic Doctrine gives us a system 'in the nearest approximate metaphor' whereby we trace the Cosmos coming into manifestation cycle by cycle and the great zodiac taking form in unlimited space. These same principles of evolution, based on the Laws of Polarity and Limitation, Equilibrium and Unbalance, are applied when we consider the creation of our Universe and of the planet Earth. These great abstract cycles, in the course of long aeons of time, became, as it were, solidified as they approached within the range of our understanding and we on our side, as consciousness evolves, reach out to grasp with the mind some straw to which we can cling, even if it is only the symbol of a reality, for the realities themselves are for the most part far beyond our mental capacity.

In the Eastern teachings on Cosmogony there is a very complicated system of planetary chains and rounds, races and sub-races, but in the West, while retaining the principles, the system has been simplified and the double evolution of the Divine Power of God coming down into matter on the one hand, and the development of the consciousness of man, rising up into unity with God on the other may be portrayed in the form of a table as follows:

	Planes			Races
7.	} Spiritual	{	Abstract	7th
6.			Concrete	6th

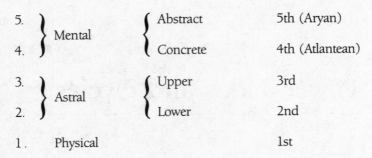

5.			Abstract	5th (Aryan)
	} Mental	{		
4.			Concrete	4th (Atlantean)
3.			Upper	3rd
	} Astral	{		
2.			Lower	2nd
1.	Physical			1st

This table may convey some impression of the cycles of human evolution Race by Race. In the 4th or Atlantean Race for instance the *mind* of humanity began to develop; the primitive man of that period was taught by the Manus of previous evolutions; and in the 5th or present Aryan Race we must learn to develop the powers of the abstract mind—to contact our higher nature. It is also taught that the cycle has come round on its orbit so that we are now touching the Atlantean contacts on a higher arc. The work of the 5th Race, however, is far from finished and it will be long before the average man will function freely on the planes of Spirit. There is much talk about the 6th Race but this talk is very premature.

Let us now consider the cycle of the Zodiac of our Universe. One round of its orbit, which is called the precession of the Equinoxes, is said to take 26,800 years, or roughly 2,200 years per sign—and again we must think spirally. At present we are nearing the conclusion of the age of Pisces, which dates from about the time of Our Lord's incarnation. There are already portents of the Aquarian age, for the states of evolution which these symbols represent overlap to a considerable extent. Each House of the Zodiac also stands for a particular type of development according to whether it is a Fire, Air, Water or Earth sign. In the age of Pisces for instance we have a Water sign corresponding to emotional development—the Christian religion is said to be a 'Water' religion, its members are admitted by baptism and its mission is Love. The Aquarian age will specialize in the development of the higher mind on the basis of Love, for it is an 'Air' sign and Air corresponds to mind. Equally the Zoroastrian religion had to do with Fire and purification by fire, and the Confucian is related to Earth.

As certain of the stations on the Qabalistic 'Tree of Life' are also referred to the Elements it is interesting to note how the Zodiac may fit on the 'Tree'.

We shall now have to adapt the principle of the Zodiac to a cycle of one year, which is divided by the two Equinoxes on the centre pillar of Equilibrium, and the two Solstices, when Sol or the Sun stands farthest from the Equator. The cycle is then divided into four quarters or two flowing and two ebbing tides.

We know that the Sun is referred to Tiphareth (No 6), the Moon to Yesod (9), the Nature Forces of the Earth to Netzach (7), and Water to Hod (8).

The Great Archangels, or Rulers of the Quadrants are also assigned to the Tree as follows: Raphael to the East (6), Gabriel to the West (9), Michael to the South (8), and Uriel to the North (7).

The Sun (6) enters Aries, a Fire sign, at the Spring Equinox on a flowing tide and the tide changes at the Summer Solstice (8) into a Water sign—Cancer. The Sun enters Libra, an Air sign, at the Autumnal Equinox (9), and ebbs at the Winter Solstice (7) with Capricorn, an Earth sign.

The Zodiac itself is a very ancient system which relates to cosmic tides, and their flow and return, but the planets correlate with states of consciousness. The Sun for instance symbolizes the Higher Self and the Moon refers more to the Personality and the etheric nature of the Earth, but it will be realized that all states of consciousness are influenced by the Cosmic tides for the Cycles of the Cosmos form the background of all manifestation.

We are also taught that there can be no manifestation without duality and we can see how duality arises from the Law of Opposites. Fire (6) and Air (9) work together; Water (8) and Earth (7) are necessary to each other. The two outer pillars of the 'Tree' represent polarizing forces. The flow and ebb of the Summer tides find their complementary opposite in the two Winter tides. Heat and cold; light and dark; form and force; spirit and matter, all is rhythmical and cyclic.

The Summer Solstice is essentially a Nature festival, especially for those who worship the sun, and its opposite—the Winter Solstice or Christmastide is a very human festival, irrespective of religious belief, whereas the Equinoxes are now much more of the nature of Church festivals, especially Easter, which is based on traditions which have their roots in a knowledge of Cosmic tides. In fact it is very interesting to note how the Early Fathers of the Church were guided to plan the Church's year on an astrological and cosmic basis.

Speaking generally, the ecclesiastical cycle commences just after the Autumnal Equinox, through Advent and the dark winter season; then we have the purification of Lent and the great uprising of all Nature at

Easter, coming to full flood at Ascension and Whitsun; then ebbing through the long period called 'after Trinity' when the experiences of the soul are stabilized. The Ember-days also mark the approach of each change of tide. They are called ember after an old Saxon word meaning circuit, and there are three before each respective Equinox and Solstice.

Referring again to the Zodiac on the 'Tree' let us trace the nature of the tides from the point of view of the Elements involved in each quarter, remembering that Fire symbolizes spirit; Air—mind; Water—emotions; and Earth—stability. From Autumn (9) when the Sun enters Libra (Air) it is a period favourable for mental work, hence so many new works are commenced then, and the Church has fixed that period for its new year—Advent. From the Winter Solstice to Spring it is a period favourable to purification which includes Lent, and we have Aquarius, the Water Bearer, and Pisces, a Water sign. From Spring to Summer we have the Sun gaining power—the Sun enters Aries, a Fire sign, and this is a period favourable to spiritual enlightenment, which includes the great Festivals of Easter, Ascension and Whitsun. And from the Summer to Autumn we gather the fruits of the Earth and usually take our holidays, prior to the commencing of another cycle—again thinking spirally.

The Rays are not strictly cyclic; they represent rather the types of consciousness symbolized by the signs of the planets. The Seven Rays are specialized aspects of the White Christ, which was 'before all worlds' and although they are all in manifestation together, yet some may predominate over others, as a particular type of consciousness evolves. The Christian Violet Ray for instance predominates in the West and the Orange robe of Buddha in the East. Broadly speaking they may be thought of as successive manifestations on the arcs of involution and evolution. The Cosmic Christ is an evolving aspect of God, and Man is an evolving aspect of Christ and must experience all the fullness of life in due course.

The red end of the spectrum is concerned with the development of the individual, and the violet end with Group Minds. The Green Ray is the connecting link—the nadir, and has affinities with both past, present and future. It is the Ray of Beauty. The Blue is the Hermetic Ray with its roots in Egypt and Chaldea; it is the Ray of the Magician. The Indigo is the Gnostic Ray of the abstract mind and of philosophy and science, and the Purple is the Ray of devotion—of healing—of the Lord Jesus.

We must think of man as being influenced by three Rays at least, for man is a triangle of emotion, mind, and spirit, and we must try to trace the relationship of one Ray with another. For instance the Green Celtic

Ray is connected with the Purple Ray through such Celtic saints as St Columba and St Bride, and with the Hermetic Ray through the Magician Merlin and the Holy Grail legends. The Indigo Ray will link with the Purple Ray through the speculations of symbolism, and much that is now dark will be brought to light by science and religion working together.

The Magician is a Priest of the Elements. He works with the powers of the Elements and Nature Forces and he is considerably affected by the changing tides. But the Lord of the Violet Ray, under whom all the Masters of the Western tradition serve in this present phase of evolution, is also Lord of the Elements, with power to command the waves and storms, as recorded in the New Testament, and as Priest of the Most High God he is much less influenced by the tides. Where the Magician would contact the Elemental Forces through their Great Regents, the ordinary Christian would do so through the Group Mind of his religion and the Lord Jesus.

Beyond the seven Rays of the spectrum and to complete its cycle there are the three Dark Rays of Destruction or disintegration when the consciousness of the planet undergoes purification and regeneration by the Powers of Darkness. These are not Powers of Evil, but rather of pure Spirit. When God said 'Let there be Light' from the darkness there dawned cycle by cycle spiritual perception, mental illumination, astral glory and the sunshine of Earth; and when the twilight sets in we must prepare for a period of evolutionary rest and refreshment before another 'Day of Brahma' commences.

Let us now consider how we can use these tides to best advantage and we will try to arrange them in orderly sequence.

There are certain tides known as Tattvas which refer to the Elements and change their aspect every twenty minutes, but their influence is so slight as to be negligible to the ordinary man. They are of value to the Magician.

The day is of course a familiar tide, and the more rhythmical our day is, the more free is consciousness, for the force of habit makes many of our actions subconscious. This is an important point with those of a contemplative nature who are desirous of contacting the higher realms, apart from the distractions and worries of ordinary life.

The week is a cycle of seven and a special planetary force is assigned to each day:

SUNDAY	—	Sun
MONDAY	—	Moon
TUESDAY	—	Mars

WEDNESDAY	—	Mercury
THURSDAY	—	Jupiter (Thor)
FRIDAY	—	Venus
SATURDAY	—	Saturn

Sunday is therefore especially a day of spiritual regeneration and Monday leads us to the next tide.

The Month is a Moon tide, for whereas the Sun refers to the Higher Self, the Moon refers to the Personality and the etheric side of the Earth. The influences of the New Moon differ from those of the Full Moon and those of the increase differ from those of the decrease. Generally speaking the rising and full moon is the more powerful for constructive work and the waning moon for destruction. The Magician is especially careful in regard to these forces.

The Quarterly Tide, from Equinox to Solstice, has a definite influence of its own and comes under its own Elemental Ruler, for each quarter is assigned to an Element, as has been shown.

The Half Yearly Tide—from Equinox to Equinox, is very important from an occult point of view, for it is often found that causes set going on the inner planes at one Equinox will take the full tide of six months to work out on the physical plane, and if we realize this we shall be content to exercise patience until the six months are accomplished.

The Year is the full round of the Astrological Signs, each with its distinctive influence. These are also gathered together into the four seasons with their triplicities. We are conscious of the rise and fall of Nature each year, even as we are of our own birthday anniversaries recurring, and we adapt ourselves accordingly. We have already noted how the Church's year has been adapted to the ancient Elemental and astrological principles.

As the Year is divided into quarters, so can a Century be divided, and it may be noted, as with the Year, so is the first quarter century the most difficult. Some of our worst wars have taken place in that period. A definite correspondence can be traced in these matters, for the same principle is involved and they vary according to the level of consciousness, whether individual, group, national, international, astral, mental etc.

The precession of the Equinoxes is a much vaster period, and a succession of Races, such as the Aryan, or Atlantean, vaster still. In fact they go far beyond the range of recorded history and we are indebted to our scientists for much of the light thrown on the matter by their research work.

Much of the information put forward in this chapter has been based on the teachings received from Adepti on the inner planes who tell us that they can co-operate with the Lords of Karma and take advantage of planetary and zodiacal conditions to arrange the circumstances of those who desire to enrol in their service after they have attained a certain stage of detachment.

10.

The Death of Vivien Le Fay Morgan

This fragment which was mediumistically received after Dion Fortune's death, is an epilogue to Moon Magic.

I am the same being who dominated Dion Fortune when she wrote *The Sea Priestess* and *Moon Magic*. I am well characterized as 'Morgan' and as 'Lilith Le Fay' in these books and I was known by many names among the ancients but today I am best described as a *persona* or magical body. I am the figure in the evolutionary background of the authoress throughout the ages.

As the time approached for me to die, I drew around myself substances of the various planes so that future occult conditions could be prepared for me as well as enabling me to withdraw from my body with ease and comfort. I had been weakening physically for some time and, realizing that I was summoned to depart, I waited unconcernedly.

I arranged to see people at certain times only and gradually this too ceased. As my faithful retainer Meatyard had died I left the household management in the hands of my friend Anita Warburn. This was the woman who had worked psychically with me in building the Temple described in *Moon Magic*. As the time of my departure approached she took up her abode downstairs and I withdrew to the Temple at the top of the house for I had decided to 'go out' there while lying on the *pastos*.

Meanwhile I had said goodbye to my priest and companion Malcolm a week beforehand but, as he was also my medical adviser, he was empowered to make the necessary practical arrangements after my withdrawal so that the corpse could be dealt with according to the custom of the time and country.

I wanted to 'go out' as we in the priesthood had done in the old days when the ritual of discarnation proceeded in stages, thus allowing the Etheric vehicle to disperse quickly and easily while the other principles were drawn at once to the Hall of Waiting.

We have to grow toward the higher Adepthood by slow and precise degrees. In this incarnation I had first worked with the sea and then with the Moon—the sea's regulator. Now, at the end, I worked in retrospect through the stages of my present life, realizing the gamut of power drawn from contemporary conditions as well as from those of the former initiations through which I had passed in my Everlasting Journey.

My body lay in a coma during the three days of this recapitulation. Then my senses returned to normal and I knew that Anita had privately consulted Malcolm and that each thought that I might even yet recover at the eleventh hour. But I myself knew that these phases of consciousness were preliminaries of death.

It was then that I saw the Priest of the Moon and I knew that I, who had always been obliged to work on my own initiative, would now be told what lay in store. The Priest of the Moon laid his hand on the great *chakra* at the crown of the head. 'Have you sufficiently considered your position?' he said. 'You brought back into this world a certain power which was to aid the present tide of evolution. Do you feel satisfied that this work is complete?' I replied, 'I have done all that I could with the tools available and have taught all that I could to those who worked with me.'

'So be it then, if you are satisfied,' came the answer, 'but think well over the matter.'

Then a terrible doubt filled my mind for I realized that there were certain teachings yet to be given and that I had not trained a successor—a *sine qua non* in occult offices. In the work of Isis that successor has to be a woman. I had no interest in women for my mission was to men. My deeper teachings also I had given to men—to Wilfred and to Malcolm— and I had left folios of documents enough to found a school. What was to be done?

The best woman for my purpose seemed Anita, for she knew my methods and had a good deal of individual power as well as energy and ambition, but I could not trust her intelligence unless she and Malcolm could join forces. Then a great silvery light flowed into the room and I knew that Isis herself would take over the case till the time of adjustment was ended. But there were misgivings in my heart, for Anita's karma was not the same as my own and her natural bent would in the end override all. I called to the Priest of the Moon and asked his advice. It drifted to me through the haze which spread round the couch: 'You have failed in part, for you have neglected an esoteric maxim and therefore there will be a penalty to pay. Yet as the work has been good in standard, it will not die, but following seeming defeat will rise again in another manner. Choose therefore the best you know to succeed in the work of Isis and, through her, do all you may towards completion; but after that you will face another death outside the earth, and then your work will enter a different stage. Try to prepare also for that stage. Farewell.'

I was desperate. My delayed training of Anita must, I realized, begin as soon as I had passed through the Hall of Waiting and was on another plane of existence—and after a time trouble would come of it. That much my intuition told me. What was the later stage of my work? It would almost certainly involve rebirth, but I felt that the Priest of the Moon also referred to another condition before that, and an interim. I had let loose the whirlwind and I had to ride it somehow. I knew, with the deep clairvoyance which precedes death, that there were three great links with the Goddess which I must clear my mind about before going: Anita, of whom I was thinking most at that time, Mollie, Wilfred's wife, for whom I had left my necklace and some instructions before I gave up the Fort. These had been put in the charge of my bankers to be given over to Wilfred later. Mollie, who had had very little chance in this life because of a strangely harsh karma, had the stuff of a High Priestess in her and later on it would be my task to train it, but that was far ahead at this time. Which was the third link? As I remembered it, my mind which was clouding over, seemed to clear miraculously. I rang the bell and when Anita rushed up I said: 'Please ask Dr Malcolm to send for Mrs Rees. She was an old friend with whom I quarrelled, but he knows her and if he says the matter is urgent, I think she will come.'

When Anita had gone, I lay back again knowing that the fourth day was now due for me to enter upon. The fifth day after the summons would be the end. If one withdraws peacefully at the appointed time, five days are spent in the final processes—processes of which the ordinary doctor is quite unaware; indeed he may even hope for a miraculous recovery in some cases. Today, since I had no more to do till my old friend should come (for I *knew* she would come) I let my intuition work on the two priests I had trained for Isis: Malcolm and Wilfred. These two were part of my work and could in their turn train others in the same way. Yet to complete my work I needed to graft it on to the Sun-forces for the patriarchal and matriarchal powers should be whole and undivided. My special work had been to stress the ancient Moon powers for healing of present day social ills in order that the profounder spiritual work could thus proceed unimpeded in the next age. It was this synthesis that modern occult schools lacked. They either used Isis in the service of Black Magic or they overstressed Osiris, breaking the Eternal Marriage of the Divine Couple. I had already many private papers of the Sun magic but the time was not yet ripe for its teaching to appear and I could not train a Sun priest for he is chosen from a certain line of Solar Succession and 'takes over' by virtue of prerogative.

The Secret Temple of Atlantis knew the worship of both Sea and Sun and the High Priestesses of Atlantis were trained by it. My work should have left the nucleus for the old Secret Temple work to continue once more in modern days. The Sun priesthood had to take up where I left off and I could but leave the matter to the Inner Chiefs when the time came, and that time would be after my withdrawal. But there floated before my closed eyes the face of a patient of Malcolm's whom I had met and who, though helped by me, had shown a curious independent enlightenment which did not come from my sources. I was able to put him in touch with his own. His name was George Brendan and while I was writing my account of the Sun magic, which is among my secret papers, I thought of Brendan constantly. That, however, is another story and anyone sufficiently interested can read all about Sun magic when and if my executors decide on its publication.

I must have lain musing on all these things for a whole day. All sense of time goes in death and in trance. I seemed to sleep for a while and then Anita brought in Lena Rees and left her beside me, after drawing up a chair to the bed.

I had not seen Lena for many years and I must now explain about her. It will be remembered that I spoke of having received my initiation in the Rue de Mozart in Paris. Lena was one of the authorities in that secret stronghold and she was, in fact, what Orientals call my *guru*. That is to say my guide or supervisor in spiritual matters. She was indeed, one of those rare beings able to appear as a successful citizen of the world—a charming, very intelligent and well-dressed woman from the point of view of the man-in-the-street—but one of the greater occultists from the point of view of the initiated. She had been of the High Priesthood in Atlantis when I myself was one of the Temple Virgins. Later on she had been of the great Priesthood of Astarte, the Syrian form of Isis. She taught me a very great deal for which I am truly grateful, but we fell out over a point on which I felt myself to be in the right and her to be in the wrong. We could not agree and as there had been the profound relationship of esoteric teacher and pupil between us, the disagreement could only end in total separation. She was the only woman for whom I had ever had a lasting liking and a deep respect. She was 'old-young' like me but not as tall and her dress was, as always, of the smartest French cut in the soft black which she preferred. She did not love colours as I did; neither would she ever wear robes except in a ritual. She could, however, bring the atmosphere of the temple into a drawing-room, above all when she spoke. Her voice was like a vibration of water heard in the distance, for she belonged to the cult of the sea and of the stars, not to that of the Moon like myself. As Lena entered she saluted the Lunar Symbol which hung above my bed. Then each made the secret manual sign by which the High Priesthood recognize each other.

'I knew you would come,' I said.

'I knew you would send for me,' she replied, 'because the time has come when you mut go on, as you have ended your work at this level.'

'Lena,' I answered, 'the difficulty is that I have done my work up to a point only, but I have left undone a great deal. I have not 'tied up the ends' and I have not prepared a successor. All that I can do is to complete my work through psychic pressure on others after my withdrawal.'

'When I began to train you,' she answered, 'I knew that there was that in you which would get carried away by its own power. We cannot do without power but it must be allied with Love or with Wisdom.'

'With Wisdom, certainly,' I said. 'We did not use Love in Atlantis in the sense that modern sentiment allots to it.'

'My dear, you have all the terror of sentimentality that the power type often has. You forget the power itself can be a form of sentimentality and that some of the cruellest men and women in history were the most sentimental.'

I agreed that what she said was true but I felt a wave of air above me and I knew that we must get down to the real business of the visit. I asked Lena if she were prepared to help me through the Barrier as had been the ancient custom, that I might the quicker pass through the Ante-Room and into the Hall of Judgment. There was a loosening of the Etheric Web and the long tenuous cable which binds the subtle vehicle to the body began to quiver and stretch almost like a snake uncoiling.

Lena leant forward: 'Can you remember the Ritual of Birth,' she said, 'for I think we should start now.'

· I replied: 'I can remember enough to make the right responses, if you will do the physical preparations. You will find symbols and lamps in the cupboard outside and robes in the little room beyond. Strange that you who first taught me of these rites, should, after a long absence, return to join me in the last one.'

Lena rose and came towards the head of the couch. She stooped to kiss me. 'I take my good-bye as friend to friend,' she said. 'I shall not be long before I also withdraw from dense matter. After all is over, I shall call Anita and she and Malcolm will see to all the worldly arrangements as you have, I hear, already arranged with them. Now I shall robe and prepare the room as we did in Atlantis. You have finished with the world and with everyday talk, for our last words will be in the language of the Mysteries.'

I reflected how strange and terrifying this scene would appear to the ordinary person. I was in full consciousness, yet feeling the body weaken and loosen minute by minute, like a skin beginning to slough off. In Atlantis we had had a ceremonial of the death-journey which prepared one for the way. The Catholics have something of the same idea in their last rites. But in those far-off days we called it the Ritual of Birth and when I was a Neophyte in Paris during this present life, we were obliged to learn and study the fragments of the secret procedure handed down through such centuries of time.

Lena returned robed in a white, gold-embroidered tunic; on her head was a striped nemyss of gold and black. She put two tall ceremonial candles on either side of my bed and extinguished the dimmed electric lamp. Behind me was a table standing a little above my head and here she lighted a floating wick in a blue bowl which shed a purplish light upon the deepening shadows. Some aromatic incense was set smouldering in a silver brazier at the far corner of the room. Then she swept up to me saying: 'I come to prepare you for the way you must go,' and draped my silver head-dress, with the Moon symbol, around my head. Over the bed she spread my own black velvet robe. The tall candles were set alight and stood like pillars on either side of me. Then she drew the great seals upon the four walls, speaking the words which invoke protection and help.

And all the time my body sank deeper into coma and my mind burned like a glowing lamp.

Lena came round and sat at the bed's foot, facing me. She raised her hand in salute. The ancient rite began.

'Behold the Goddess forms in the East,' said Lena.

'I am withdrawn into her hands,' I answered.

'The floods uplift the Barge of thy outgoing,' said she.

'Waft thou my soul down the River of Naradek,' said I.

'Cast thou thy cerements into my hands,' Lena replied.

'Lo, I unwind the shroudings of life and cast them into thy hands,' I murmured.

Lena rose, holding out her hands, like a statue of Nephthys of Egypt, and making gestures to the four quarters of the universe: 'I cast thy shrouds to the winds and waters. I cast thy shrouds to the flames and to the earth.' She sat down again.

And now a great force stirred behind me in the East and I began to rise up the whole length of my body towards the shadowy form of the Goddess standing there. A film of moonlight spread over all the atmosphere and my Etheric web seemed to be ripped from me and to disperse towards the four cardinal points.

A vast tide seemed surging under me as though I were being carried in a barge down a rushing stream into the West.

Still Lena's words went on with the age-old and ever familiar words:

'Helios, Helios shine thou upon her,
Bring her to Light and to Life and to Love . . .'

I watched in a dim way behind my eyes for they were ceasing to function. The sense of smell too was very weak and the incense seemed to have burnt out. Yet one supreme sense—not of the body—showed me that I was standing rather unsteadily just outside the quiet form on the couch and that the smoke from the silver brazier still rose in clouds with occasional sparks leaping up into the gloom.

Lena was making curious motions with her hands as though she were unravelling a skein. She chanted:

'Lo, I unravel the vesture which Thou in the East didst weave: Thy priestess passes out to thee, O my Sister. She is clothed with the power. She shines within thy form. Thy priestess is born from Thee O Mother. Cut thou the Silver Cord of Birth.'

And then there was a curious jerk and the tenuous Etheric line between soul and body broke. I entered upon the inner planes and seemed to glow with a great brilliance for an instant, within the body of Isis—for this is the higher Birth.

Lena saw me for she was strongly psychic. She rose and stood upright raising her hands to the Moon Symbol. Then she stopped and closed the eyes of the body on the bed and made the seals of the Sons of Horus and left the room in silence.

I knew that she had gone to tell Anita to summon Malcolm. I was free. The powerful ritual had dispersed the Etheric at once, instead of the usual hanging around for three days in the atmosphere of funeral arrangements. The Priest of the Moon came to me, 'Come now to the place of waiting,' he said, 'and then you will rest for a while till full strength is renewed.' 'And then?' said I. 'Then you will pass to the Hall of Osiris and your heart will be weighed in the balance and you will kneel before the crook and flail and Isis and Nephthys will stand behind you and Anubis will guide you and you will know that each of these great symbols is a part of yourself and you will be your own judge.'

'There are those who shirk the Judgment and those who brace themselves to know the verdict of God who speaks within their own spirit. Which are you?' And I answered 'I want to know the verdict and if I can, to continue with some work left undone.' 'You will know that later,' he replied.

Then I sank into a deep rest—a sleep within a sleep . . .

(A strong, deep line now seemed drawn across the paper.)

Index